VOLUME

4

REAL ESTATE INVESTING

Seller Finance

Library of Congress In Publication Data
October 2004

Txu-1-204-543

Real Estate Seller Finance

10 9 8 7 6 5 4 3 2 1

The enclosed material is designed for educational purposes only. Each State may have different certification and specific guidelines. Please refer to your State for additional and future information. The information contained herein is considered correct at the time of creation but laws and regulations are updated frequently and the reader assumes the responsibility for confirming current regulations and applicable data. The publisher and author make no warranty as to the success of the individuals using the training material contained herein. The publisher and author make no warranty as to any action taken by any individual completing this program. The reader is responsible for the appropriate use of the materials and information provided. This publication is designed to provide accurate and authoritative information concerning the subject matter. All material is sold with the understanding that neither the author nor the publisher guarantees the actions of any individual making use of the inclusions. Neither the author nor the publisher is rendering a legal opinion, accounting recommendation or other professional service. If legal advice or other expert assistance is desired, the services of a legal professional or other individual should be sought. **The applicable federally released forms, disclosures and notices are generated from public domain. Copyright law does apply to all intellectual materials and all rights under said law are reserved b y the copyright owner.**

Coursework is available at special quantity discounts to use as premiums and sales promotions within corporate or private training programs. To obtain information or inquire about availability please write to Director, PO Box 1, Hollidaysburg, PA 16648.

NOTICE

REAL ESTATE INVESTING

Seller Finance

Creative financing options present an incredible opportunity to anyone involved in real estate transactions. Whether you are a buyer, a seller, an investor or even a real estate professional, a comprehensive understanding of creative financing and the opportunities it provides can allow you to obtain your goals much more quickly and more simply than nearly any other opportunity in the real estate or personal investment arenas today.

- **Sellers**   will learn how to sell their properties much more quickly, with fewer hassles and headaches and for MORE money than ever before.

- **Buyers**   any buyers, regardless of their personal situation, can fulfill their dreams of homeownership now. With less up-front money, fewer credit guidelines and a simpler transaction than with other financing and purchase options available in the conventional market.

- **Investors**   can leverage more real estate than ever before building their cash flow, return on investment and net worth in ways never before imagined.

- **Real Estate Agents**   can benefit from a comprehensive understanding of creative financing techniques by learning how to sell more homes, more quickly and to more buyers than ever before.

Creative financing is defined as financing that falls outside the standard conventional financing offered by banks and lending institutions.

This course is designed to aid you in understanding what types of financing are commonly negotiated and provide the information you need to convert these tried and true methods for use in your personal situation.

The materials will provide you with a crash course in private finance that will enable you to customize your negotiations around your specific needs.

You will gain the upper hand in any negotiation process by obtaining the knowledge needed to have a full understanding of the perspective of the other party!

Regardless of the part you plan to take in the transaction, you should read each section carefully. The material covered will provide you with vital information that will enable you to successfully negotiate the deal in a manner that is beneficial to you.

Creative financing is typically a synonym for seller financing. Seller financing and seller assistance are common terms that you will hear in your market.

Seller financing simply means that the seller is willing to hold the paper or mortgage on a piece of real estate in a manner similar to the methods used by the banking industry.

- The seller receives the down payment, monthly principal installments and best of all the interest for the sale of the real estate.

- The seller is able to obtain a higher profit than they would have with a flat sale.

- The seller is typically able to sell their property much more quickly than they would if they required the buyers obtain the purchase funds from another source.

- Selling the property using creative financing can provide an additional financial benefit through tax breaks, deferment of tax payments and interest received.

These same benefits have made the banking industry so profitable. Now, as a seller, you will have the ability to profit just as the banks always have and to sell your home in days not months!

- Buyers are able to fulfill their dreams of homeownership more quickly than with conventional methods. This can be accomplished even when the buyer has special situations like a low down payment, past or present credit issues, even job interruptions or high debt loads.

- Buyers will also typically pay far less in closing costs utilizing seller financing because there is less paperwork, no loan officer commission to pay and fewer requirements and restrictions involved in the process.

Many potential homeowners mistakenly believe that just because the banks say no, their dreams of owning a home of their own must die. Now everyone CAN be a homeowner with all of the security and self-respect homeownership provides faster and with less up-front money than ever before.

- Investors will be able to leverage more property more quickly because they will not have to comply with strict down payment requirements for non-owner occupied property, debt ratio limitations or even limits on how many properties they are allowed to finance.

- PLUS an investor obtains all of the benefits of any other buyer – less down money, looser guidelines and fewer closing costs.

- Creative financing offers the intelligent and informed investor the opportunity to increase their cash flow, net worth and cash on cash leverage much more quickly than any other financing option available.

Real estate investment has provided more Americans with the means of achieving millionaire status than any other opportunity. This course will teach you to capitalize on the exciting opportunities available through Creative finance. Once you have mastered this course, there are others available which will teach you how to increase your net worth and monthly cash flow quickly and effectively.

- Real estate professionals will learn how to increase their income by selling more of their listed homes. Some of the listings in the files may not qualify for conventional lending programs but will sell quickly using creative finance techniques.

- The newly trained real estate agent will be able to work with more buyers who may not qualify under any lending programs and to take these buyers to closing more quickly than with any other finance option.

- Lending guidelines sometimes make obtaining financing and ultimately a closing on some of your listings a difficult process. Now you can close more listings than ever before.

    The property may be devalued due to excessive land ratios.

    The loan to value may be lowered because the property is rural.

    The property may require extensive and costly renovations to fulfil the underwriting requirements of a particular loan program.

Every real estate professional realizes there are be some properties in the listing files that just cannot transfer in the conventional market. Now, with the seller holding the paper, the buyer has the opportunity to build equity to offset reduced valuation or loan to value ratios.

The buyer may buy the property "as is" and perform renovations in their own time which will satisfy the lender guidelines and help increase the value of the property for refinance.

All of these factors and others that will be detailed later aid you in learning how to close more homes in your listing file than ever before.

- A thorough understanding of creative finance, the willingness to be creative in negotiations and the ability to assist both sellers and buyers in the process offers Real Estate Agents the opportunity to work with more buyers than ever before.

  Up to 40% of the potential homebuyers in your area have characteristics that keep them from qualifying for conventional lending programs.

  Now, you can work with those same buyers who would have been written off because of a lack of finance.

  You can get them into homes now rather than years from now.

  This course teaches you how to offer the keys that will fulfill your buyer's dreams today and to increase your income and reputation by up to 40% this year!

  When you take the increased closings stimulated by working with more buyers and sellers and add in the reputation you will gain in your region as the Real Estate Agent who thinks outside the box, you will have found the key that can drive you to top agent status.

- Word of mouth referrals are known as the best advertisement you can obtain. The one advertisement that cannot be bought.

  By gaining background knowledge in creative finance to add to your service repertoire, you are placing yourself in the center of a transaction that other Agents in your area cannot negotiate.

  You will create a win-win situation for both your buyers and your sellers and they will spend years telling how you aided them in obtaining the deal of their life.

  No advertising budget can buy you that kind of publicity!

Creative finance creates a win-win situation for any party involved who is willing to remain open minded and flexible in negotiations. This is truly one of the most important courses you will ever read!

Creative or Seller Financing is known by many names. Each of the terms used will have one thing in common, the transactions financial arrangements remain private between individual buyers and sellers. This allows for a much greater flexibility for each party in the negotiations. This increased flexibility and opportunity to negotiate on key points that are important to each party provides the potential for huge financial benefits to all parties involved in a transaction.

Many people believe that all of the terms used to describe creative finance are interchangeable but the reality is that each term varies slightly in the process of finance and the conditions of the contract. Before you begin the search for a property and a motivated buyer or seller, it is important that you understand the variations so that you can speak intelligently and avoid confusion.

Understanding the common variations currently in use in the market will also allow you to custom design your transaction to fulfill all of your goals.

The first step in understanding creative finance is to obtain a basic knowledge of the common types of transactions currently popular and the terms used to describe these transactions. As you read through the descriptions and later the details of the common transactions, it is important to remember that creative finance is just that – creative. You can structure your transaction to suit your needs. Do not feel limited by the common programs described. The methods of finance in this course popularized by normal people just like you. These people needed a particular benefit or situation and were not afraid to ask. There are hundreds of variations to the programs described in this course. Each variation may provide additional benefits for you and your situation.

In a creative finance transaction, you are only limited by your imagination, some basic real estate transfer laws and your ability to show the other party how beneficial the negotiation points you want included in the transaction can be for all of the parties involved.

Land contract, Article of Agreement, Option, Lease Option, Contract for Deed, Installment Contract. These are all common terms used to describe the creative finance technique. They all have the similar characteristic of being privately enacted between the buyer and the seller but there most of the similarity ends. Each of these terms actually carries very different specific connotations that most people who believe they have a firm grasp of creative financing techniques fail to comprehend. This course will enable you to differentiate the variations and use them to your advantage.

1

CHAPTER

Commonly Negotiated Deals

A contract for deed or installment contract, sometimes also called a land contract, has been used primarily for the purchase of land parcels. The finance of raw land is a difficult transaction to complete using the more conventional lending options. Because of this difficulty, sellers and buyers began financing this type of purchase independent of the financial institutions. This method of finance was so successful with land transactions that today, many improved real estate transactions or actual sales of homes and investment properties use the same premise of sale.

The land contract or installment contract is one of the most common methods of seller finance.

This is a relatively straightforward form of seller finance that is easy to negotiate and well understood by most of the parties involved.

The term land contract or installment contract is a simple contract where the terms are negotiated and the buyer makes payments to the seller.

The seller acts as a mortgagor and handles activities typically completed by a banking institution

- collect payments

- amortize the transaction

- handle escrow if applicable

- confirm property tax payments

- confirm hazard insurance coverage's

- completes any other function normally fulfilled by a conventional lender.

These contracts are the basis for nearly every other contract outlined in the book.

Each variation created through negotiation changes the terminology used to describe the transaction.

A contract for deed is a scenario where the title or deed to the property is actually retained by the seller until all conditions of the sale such as are met. These conditions may include items such as:

- Full payment of all purchase money

- Receipt of all accrued interest

- Any other negotiated items agreed to between the parties

This type of finance allows for a higher amount of security on the part of the seller since the deed is not transferred on record to the buyer until after the sale terms are complete.

This limits the hassles and processes involved in case of a default by the buyer.

From both parties' perspective, this method of finance is beneficial because it defers the need to pay transfer tax and most recording fees as well as other costs until the transaction is complete.

It is important to check with your local government to ensure the compliance with all regulations regarding this type of transaction.

It is also beneficial to obtain the services of a competent legal professional for assistance with the details.

Transaction Details and Benefits

Deed Escrow: From the buyers perspective it may become a negotiation point to escrow the deed with an attorney or other third party that can act on the part of the seller.

This ensures the finalization processes occur in a timely manner if, for some reason, the seller is unable to finalize the process after the buyer has fulfilled his obligations.

Down Payment: In this method of finance, the buyer and seller will typically negotiate a down payment that is acceptable to both parties.

The down payment allows the seller to feel a certain security has been invested on the part of the borrower.

This investment aids in preventing default on the loan terms and condition.

Monthly Payments: Regular monthly payments are typically set.

These will usually pay down the principal portion of the loan balance.

Monthly payments will often include an amortized interest payment.

At times, the loan may be negotiated as an interest only transaction.

> Monthly payments in an interest only transaction do not reduce the principal balance owed.

> Monthly payments in an interest only transaction are credited only toward interest accrued on the principal balance.

An escrow or amount to be held for the payment of taxes and insurance is sometimes incorporated into the monthly payment.

Interest Rate: Interest is typically included as part of the negotiation process.

> The rate of interest will be set at a level, which insures profitability to the seller and is manageable and fair to the buyer.

Interest is completely contingent on the needs of both parties and will typically be set at a rate higher than the prime rate offered by conventional lenders.

Important information regarding the negotiation of the interest rate and the effect interest rate can have on each party is included later in the book.

A section concerning how lenders price a loan product is also included and may assist both the buyer and the seller in reaching a mutual decision concerning interest on the private mortgage.

Escrows: If the seller agrees to accept monthly "escrow" payments toward the payment of the real estate property taxes and the homeowner's insurance premiums, the seller is then acting as an escrow servicer to the loan.

He must set up an escrow account, which will enable the bills to be paid in a timely manner.

He must comply with all escrow account rules and regulations.

An escrow account allows the funds toward the payment of taxes and insurance to be set-aside in a dedicated account.

Placing these funds in a secure account allows the tax and insurance bills to be paid in a timely manner and provides security to both parties.

At times, a buyer may agree to make the real estate property tax and homeowner's insurance premium payments as they come due.

It is vital that these bills are paid according to the terms agreed. A delay or actual non-payment of these bills can put the interests of both the buyer and the seller in jeopardy.

OPTION TO PURCHASE

Many people confuse the term "option" with the term "lease with the option to purchase". These terms are similar in some ways but vary greatly in the conditions of negotiation and even the responsibilities of both parties.

An option is simply the first right to purchase a property. In the transfer of improved real estate, options are not used as frequently as some of the other creative finance methods.

Options are used to extend the period of decision on whether to purchase a property or piece of land.

Example: A time when the use of an option would be beneficial is when a large tract of land is being sold.

If a seller has 100 acres of land available and wishes to sell it to a developer, the seller may be asked to hold an option on a portion of the property.

Issue: The developer may be unable to afford the entire parcel at the present time.

The developer may wish to conduct a marketability study using only a portion of the acreage to determine if his current market has room for the development of the full parcel.

Solution: The developer may purchase a smaller portion, for example 25 acres, and request an option to purchase the remaining acreage after a certain period of time.

A stipend or financial payment to the seller typically accompanies this option request.

This payment compensates the seller for the period they are unable to sell their land and provides security that the developer is serious about the eventual purchase.

In consideration of the financial stipend the developer is given the time to

o   sub-divide the acreage he did purchase

o   develop a sub-division or individual homes upon the land

o   determine exactly how much of a need there is for a larger area of development in his community

The developer is also given more time to arrange for the finance of the remaining acreage, either through the sale of the newly constructed homes on the first portion of land purchased or with a conventional lending source, investor or other provider of funds.

Nullification   In the event the developer chooses not to purchase the remaining parcel of land, he is released from all obligations to the seller limiting the financial jeopardy to his overall business.

The seller typically retains the stipend paid at the original option signing as compensation for the time lost.

REAL ESTATE INVESTING – SELLER FINANCE

The seller can then market the remaining portion of his land to another buyer. This situation provides limited risk to both parties.

Completion   If the developer does wish to exercise his option to purchase, the handling of the stipend or option premium is subject to negotiation between the developer and the seller.

Whether the seller keeps the stipend as a repayment for the decision time granted or whether this stipend is credited back to the developer toward the overall purchase costs is often a key negotiating point in the early stages of the transaction.

There are other reasons an individual might use an option agreement. This is an example of one very common use. The scenario in which you find yourself may require an option.

Options are not limited to the purchase and sale of raw land only. An option might be put into place for other types of real estate and the above scenario can be modified to suit your situations.

Examples of option agreements and applicable forms are included later in the manual under the chapter headed understanding contracts.

LEASE WITH THE OPTION TO BUY

A lease with the option to buy is a creative financing technique between the landlord and the tenant of a property.

Example   The tenant agrees to rent the property for a certain period of time on the condition that he is allowed to convert his lease to a purchase agreement.

This condition fulfils the option portion, in other words the tenant obtains the option to purchase.

This method allows the tenant-buyer a term to assess his ability to manage the responsibility of homeownership.

The buyer will sometimes use this option term as an opportunity to change his personal situation to comply with the underwriting guidelines for conventional loan programs.

A buyer may desire an option term in order to gain the time he may need to save an adequate down payment for the purchase of the property.

The landlord-seller is guaranteed a certain amount of rent during the lease option.

The seller will usually secure a potential buyer for his property much more quickly than he would if other methods were used.

Often lease-options provide the seller with a higher then market average rent for his property during the option period.

Another benefit to the landlord-seller is that the tenant-buyer will have an enhanced interest in maintaining the property than other tenants.

This elevated interest is a result of the fact that at the end of the lease term the tenant-buyer may actually own the property.

This potential ownership will typically cause the tenant-buyer to treat the property more carefully and perform basic functions.

The tenant-buyer's vested interest in the property provides more security concerning the retention of value and the condition of their property to a seller than a straight rental agreement.

This factor weighs heavily with property owners who must sell their property for a variety of reasons but are hesitant to rent the property due to the potential for a decrease in value or damage to the property.

Lease with option to buy agreements are typically set up so that the potential buyer pays an amount in excess of the standard rental payment for similar properties in the area.

The landlord-seller will usually keep the excess payment if the tenant-buyer chooses not to exercise his option to buy at the end of the guarantee option term or lease agreement.

If the tenant-buyer does exercise the option to purchase within the set option period, the amount of excess money paid to the landlord-seller is often credited as down payment money when the final sales agreement is negotiated.

If the tenant-buyer is attempting to secure conventional financing for the purchase, the underwriter in charge of approving the buyer's loan application uses certain guidelines concerning the option payments. Most lenders will allow the use of the surplus lease option payments toward the buyer's down payment requirements providing a couple of basic criteria are met.

The amount of the monthly payment that can be used toward down payment must often be more than the standard rent for the area.

Example: If the standard rent for a property in the area similar to the one being sold, is $300 and the tenant-buyer who held the lease option paid $450 per month in consideration of the option, the excess $150 dollars may often be utilized as down payment.

Amount paid $450 – Standard rent $300 = Down payment credit $150.

Down payment credit $150 x Months paid 12 = Down payment acceptable to underwriting $1800.

Example: If the same tenant-buyer holding an option for the same property only paid the $250 a month, which is less than the standard rental costs of the same type property in the area the underwriter would typically not allow any of the paid funds to be sourced as part of the tenant-buyers down payment requirement.

This underwriter decision is based upon the fact that according to standard rents for the area, the tenant-buyer's monthly payments only paid the seller for the rental and provided no additional funds toward the option-purchase.

Another standard requirement from underwriting when dealing with two individuals is that the transfer of all funds must be verified through an independent third party. The underwriting theory is that a personal party receipt can be easily falsified whereas cancelled checks or deposit slips showing funds placed in a bank account cannot.

It is beneficial to both parties to plan the eventual conventional refinance or lease option purchase at the time of the initial lease-option negotiation. This planning enables all of the parties to take the appropriate steps to ensure a smooth transition to conventional finance.

PARTIAL FINANCING OR SELLER 2ND

The discussion of underwriting guidelines and requirements brings us to another common use of seller financing. At times, a seller and buyer may find it beneficial to finance only a portion of the sales price of a property privately.

Most buyers and even many conventional mortgage loan officers fail to note an important condition inherent in many loan product approvals. This condition states that if the loan to value obtained by the buyer is below a certain percentage then none or only a small portion of the buyer's down payment must be sourced – or proven to be the buyers own money.

Example: A conventional approval for a 95% LTV or an agreement on the part of the bank to finance 95% of the sales price of the property may require the buyer to put 5% of their own funds towards the purchase price of that property.

Sales Price – LTV Approval = Down payment of borrower funds

When we say the buyers own funds we mean the funds that the buyer must prove as funds out of their own pocket, not a gift or loan toward the purchase.

A condition that is often overlooked in this type of approval is that if the approval allows for a 95% LTV and only an 80% LTV is accepted by the buyer there is no need to source the buyer's funds.

$$\text{Sales Price} - \text{Minimized LTV} = \text{Seller Financed } 2^{nd}$$

The theory on the part of the lending institution is that the buyer was a decent risk at the higher loan to value offered and is therefore a minimal risk if a lower loan to value is accepted.

These numbers are examples and each loan will carry different guidelines. A competent loan officer will be able to tell you what the percentage cut off is for a particular loan concerning the sourced funds requirement.

Example: Pertinent to this type of creative financing, if the seller agrees to hold a 2nd mortgage against the property in this example, 20% of the sales price, the bank will provide the 80% of the sales price as a loan on the part of the buyer to the seller immediately.

The seller then receives a cash out balance equal to 80% of the sales price and receives principal plus interest payments monthly toward the financed 20% of the sales price.

Sales Price	$100,000		
Mortgage	$ 80,000	(80% LTV)	Seller Lump Sum Payment
Seller 2nd	$ 20,000	(20% LTV)	Seller Monthly Payment

The receipt of principal plus interest payments can dramatically increase the overall profit the seller receives for the property.

The buyers are typically not required to use any of their own funds to purchase the property.

This underwriting loophole makes the transaction easier to manage for many buyers and the seller receives monthly payments of principal PLUS INTEREST until their portion of the mortgage is satisfied.

This option allows for a cash-out to the seller of a large portion of the sales price.

This cash-out is often enough liquid funds to enable the seller to fulfill their financial needs.

The seller receives the added benefit of a regular monthly payment and the opportunity to earn increased money from their property through the addition of interest.

Interest accumulation can truly benefit the seller. Interest accumulations and the effect these payments can have on the seller's bottom line are covered in the section concerning seller benefits later in the book.

- The option of obtaining a conventional first mortgage combined with a seller held second mortgage allows more buyers to qualify for conventional financing than would otherwise be possible.

- This option also gives the buyer the opportunity to retain their cash for needed repairs to the property or the purchase of furniture and other items.

- Another important benefit to the buyer is that by financing through the bank only 80% of the sales price the requirement to carry Private Mortgage Insurance is typically removed.

> Private mortgage insurance is charged on many mortgages if the amount financed exceeds 80% of the value of the property.

> The reason for the private mortgage insurance is that until the buyer has invested 20% of their money or holds a 20% equity position in the property, the possibility of default is higher.

> Private Mortgage Insurance protects the bank from heavy losses if the buyer should default.

> It does not provide any true benefit to the buyer beyond the ability to obtain a higher loan to value on the property and can be quite costly.

Private Mortgage Insurance does serve a purpose if you do not understand the concepts of creative financing.

> Private mortgage insurance is a method that allows lenders to offer home loans to borrowers with a minimum amount of equity security.

With a properly negotiated creative financing scenario coupled with fully informed parties the need for the higher loan to value and therefore the private mortgage insurance is negated.

Most loan officers will not think to offer this finance opportunity, either because they lack knowledge of creative finance tactics or because they are simply used to one method of structuring a loan package. However, most loan officers will jump at the opportunity to close an extra loan this month with fewer headaches than a high LTV loan program creates.

Real estate professionals should carefully review this creative finance scenario. Many potential closings are lost each year due to a lack of down payment funds on the part of the buyer or an inability to meet source of funds requirements as set by underwriting guidelines. Aiding in the negotiation of a seller held 2nd mortgage is an opportunity to create more closings for you and to improve your reputation as the Real Estate Agent who can structure and close any deal!

2

CHAPTER

Negotiation Process

Now that you understand the basic terms used to describe the most commonly used contracts of creative finance transactions, it is important that you understand the negotiation process.

Each variation negotiated between the buyer and the seller will alter

- the transaction type

- the terms used to describe the transaction

- the contracts of the transaction

The variations will be the custom designed negotiation points, which will make the use of creative financing techniques a benefit to every party involved in the transaction.

Regardless of your position in the transaction, you will want to understand the key components of the deal from the perspective of every party involved.

This understanding will aid you, not only in obtaining your key negotiation goals, but also in selling the other party on the benefits of those negotiation points.

Each point carries benefits to both parties and if you focus on the points in a manner that tells the other party "what's in it for me" you will discover that you have a fantastic negotiation skill whose potential you have never before tapped.

Any successful negotiator or sales person will tell you that the key to a successful transaction is to allow the other party to perceive the benefits of the deal for them.

- You must understand what you want, but the other party is not sitting at that negotiation table to fulfill your dreams.

- The other party is there to obtain the best possible scenario for them.

- It is your job to outline the benefits you desire in a manner that shows the other party why these points are benefits to them.

The next chapter will outline for you the perspective of both the buyer and the seller.

1. You should carefully review the benefits from your perspective to determine what points you must obtain.

2. Then take that list and determine how those same points can benefit the other party.

3. Expend your focus during the negotiation on those factors that that you must obtain but focus using the other parties perspective.

   Any time you can show the benefit the other party will receive by fulfilling your needs, you have an agreement from that other party.

Benefits of "what's in it for me?" negotiation

- A seller can better negotiate the sales price, interest rate and terms if he has an adequate understanding of the benefits a buyer may receive and the terms that will be desirable for a buyer.

- A buyer can better negotiate if he fully comprehends the benefits a seller will receive by using creative financing to sell their property and can sufficiently sell these benefits to the seller.

- An investor must be able to convincingly negotiate an agreement for financing that a seller will find beneficial while at the same time retaining as much financial leverage as he can to create a higher cash flow and stronger equity position for his investment portfolio.

To gain the upper hand in any negotiation process, to obtain the most desirable terms for YOU, you must completely understand the positioning of the other party.

Negotiating in creative finance is the same as any negotiation activity – always highlight the benefits and features that are important to you from the perspective of the other party.

You must think of the transaction in the same way the other party thinks.

This will allow you to consider the negotiations from the perspective of the other party to gain a through understanding of what they need, want, desire and most importantly, what objections they may make to your needed negotiating points.

Knowing what objections may arise before they do will allow you to plan an answer strategy that effectively negates the objection. More about handling objections is contained later in the chapter.

Understanding the thoughts of the other party and being able to emphasize key components of the deal that will benefit the other party while downplaying components that are most important to you will allow you to negotiate every transaction to reach a successful outcome that provides you with all of the most important requirements you need for a beneficial transaction.

The theory we practice is to downplay the importance of the components of the negotiation that are most important to you. This ability to downplay the importance of these points while focusing attention on other factors that are not as important will allow you to obtain a concession or agreement on your important factors.

You will also appear to provide all of the concessions to the other party in the form of agreements with their desired terms. These agreements will center on the components that are less important to you.

As you review the following chapters, you will see that many of the negotiation points carry benefits to both parties. Your job in the negotiation is to determine which benefits are most important to you and to negotiate toward those points. To negotiate toward those points, simply make a list of your goals and then review the same points in the chapter designed for the other party. You can then walk into the negotiation with a full listing of key considerations that you can show the other party, pointing out the benefits they receive from each point.

When negotiating always remember that regardless of your position in the transaction you are selling the deal. A sales person would not walk into a sales meeting and say "buy this because the commission is higher for me if you do" he would walk in knowing that he will obtain that commission, promptly forget about the commission and then focus only on the products benefits to the buyer!

Building Rapport

The first step to any successful negotiation meeting is to build rapport with the other party. Building rapport increases the other party's confidence in you and helps put them at ease. It is much easier to negotiate terms and conditions when both parties are relaxed and amiable.

Keys to Rapport

Listen	Two ears, one mouth for a reason!
	It is very important to be a good listener.
	Listen for statements involving their family, their work, or recreational activities. Knowing about the other party allows you to converse on subjects that are interesting to them and to help put them at ease. Understanding something of their private life may also provide important clues as to the goals and needs of the other party.
3rd Parties	Use scenarios with your own relatives or friends involved such as; "yes, my dad used to do that…" or You know I had an old college buddy that used to live in that area…"
Flattery	Used sparingly, flattery can be very effective at keeping a prospect interested.
	You must come across as sincere or the effect could be negative!
	Example: A retired person tells you they are retired. "No, Mr.//Ms. _____, you don't look old enough to be retired. You must have retired early!
	Example: A female tells you that she is unemployed or is a housewife. " Well, you have the toughest kind of full-time job! My grandmother used to tell me she worked 36 hours a day 8 days a week…."
Conclusion	These are only a few examples of how you can build rapport. The only limit is your imagination and enthusiasm!

Problems to Avoid in Rapport Building

- Do not overuse rapport. You will lose focus of your objective if you get too close to the prospect.

- Do not be patronizing with your comments.

- Do not be afraid or too timid to ask questions (it will show through.)

- Do not cut someone off in the middle of a sentence.

- Do not lose control of the meeting!

The Negotiation Meeting

If you are negotiating only one creative finance transaction, the negotiation meeting may not be as vital as it would if you are an investor or another person with multiple transactions to negotiate. If you are planning to use creative techniques frequently, it is important to have an overview of the goals of the meeting before leaving your office.

This overview is an outline of what you wish to accomplish during the meeting. You should take the following checklist with you on each meeting, allowing you to stay on the program and to review your performance immediately following the call. Reviewing your performance allows for constant improvement making each effort more effective.

GOAL   COMMENTS

- Create Rapport   _____

- Clarify financing needs   _____

- Make a general benefit statement   _____

  Personal Selling Statement   _____

- Make a transition statement   _____

  To help you transaction to suit
  your needs I need to review with you...   _____

- Explain briefly what YOU can DO   _____

- Summarize information presented and review _____
  what you can do for them
  (Avoid discussing rate and transaction specifics)_____

- Discuss transaction and pricing options   _____

  Focus on solving a problem – minimizing   _____

down payment, moving quickly etc.   _____

- If objections are present deal with them   _____

- Ask for the transaction   _____

  Summarize benefits   _____

  Get commitment to buy/sell   _____

- Conclude call and outline the next steps   _____

MEETING PREPARATION

One of the biggest fears we have is the fear of public speaking. There are preparatory tasks you can complete to reduce your internal tension when presenting an agenda.

1. Know the agenda.

   Each meeting or presentation has certain goals that the meeting must address.

   Preparing an agenda that incorporates all of these goals will allow you to maintain a focus on these goals and maintain a consistent flow.

   You will be able to control the meeting minimizing outside discussions and address all essential materials.

2. Research the topics.

   You must know what materials must be addressed during the meeting so that you are certain all vital negotiation points are covered.

3. Memorize your opening.

   The most difficult task of public speaking is to begin. Once you start your meeting your preparation will enable you to relax into the flow of your agenda.

   Before entering the meeting or presentation always review the first few sentences of your agenda or speech so that they will flow naturally off your tongue. Once you have made it through the first few sentences, you will find that your knowledge of the agenda and preparation allow the remainder of the meeting to flow smoothly.

4. Take a deep breath.

   Deep breathing will assist you with three vital functions when speaking.

   Before entering the meeting, you should spend a few seconds performing a deep breathing exercise.

   Inhale slowly through your nose.

   Hold the breath for a few seconds.

   Exhale slowly through your mouth.

   Repeat this process until your nervous tension begins to dissipate.

   The focus you place on the breathing exercise will reduce your ability to focus on the performance you must give.

   Deep breathing reduces nervous tension and supplies additional oxygen flow to your body providing greater relaxation.

   Taking a deep breath before entering the room will enable you to begin speaking with few pauses. This ensures a flow and confidence to your opening statements that will capture the attention of your negotiation partner and enhance your feelings of confidence.

   Taking a deep breath before speaking adds depth and power to your voice.

   This will assist you in maintaining the attention of the other individuals in the meeting.

   A deep and powerful voice projects confidence and gains attention.

   If you do not have an adequate air supply, your voice will sound weak and mousy.

   A weak mousy voice shows a lack of confidence and will quickly cause those listening to you to lose interest.

5. Speak slowly and clearly.

   A slow, well-modulated voice will project an aura of confidence that causes others to listen more closely to what you are saying.

Later we will tell you to vary your pace and your pitch to emphasize important points but you should always return to a slow, clear and well-modulated tone to ensure you project confidence to your listeners.

Speaking too quickly and allowing your words to run together shows your nervousness and causes others to strain to understand what you are saying.

6. Smile before you begin speaking.

You convey the expression on your face in your voice.

A smile on your face and in your voice serves to relax both you and those to whom you are speaking.

Entering the room and beginning your discussion with a smile will generate a relaxed feeling and enthusiastic response from those in the meeting and in your own mind.

7. Present the appropriate appearance.

Confidence is linked to how other people view you. It is difficult to project confidence if your appearance is not appropriate. Others base their decisions concerning your abilities and character on the appearance you present to the world. Most people will form their opinions of you within the first thirty seconds of meeting you.

Knowing you present the appropriate appearance to the world and project the impression you desire will go a long way toward building your confidence and reducing the nervousness you feel in negotiation situations.

Tips for Overcoming Objections

- Diffuse an objection before it is raised.

   The best way to overcome an objection is to incorporate both the objection and its solution into your discussion.

   "Now that we have discussed this option, you should know that..."

   "This point actually allows us to…"

   "Which ensures that you get ..."

- When an unanticipated objection is voiced, listen intently to it.

  Ask questions if you do not understand both the objection and the motivation behind it.

  Then rephrase the objection in an accepting manner.

  > "So, if I understand you, you feel... Is that correct?"

  > "And you feel that is important because..."

- Compliment the objector.

  Acknowledge the wisdom of an objection without being patronizing.

  > "That is an interesting thought/unique insight."

- Remain calm.

  Always attack the objection NOT the objector.

  Avoid showing fear or anxiety.

  Maintain your enthusiasm.

  > "I like the idea that you are thinking of the contract in those terms. Let me show you what else we might do..."

- Throw the objection back.

  Ask for the reason behind the objection.

  > "So, you think... why is that?"

- Win a series of small battles in order to win the war.

  Get agreement on other issues that lead you to overcoming the objection.

  > "So, we did agree on...?

  > "And we agreed that... was important?"

"And of course... is quite necessary in your sale?"

- Answer the objection.

  Show why your idea is not negated by the objection

  "The purpose of that particular point is to ensure you get... so you see that point actually works in your favor."

- If resistance continues, aid the objector in overcoming his/her own objection.

  "That is an interesting dilemma. How did other potential buyers deal with that?"

  " What are their disadvantages?"

  "Overall, can you see how our offer with ... is more advantageous you in the long run?"

3

CHAPTER

The Seller's Position

Creative financing holds many benefits for a seller.

Speed of Sale: In a soft real estate market offering creative or seller held financing might allow the seller to sell their property more quickly than other real estate in the area and for a higher average sales price!

This occurs because there are more buyers to source when the seller offers seller finance. The expanded market exists because up to 40% of all potential homebuyers do not qualify for conventional bank finance programs.

Sell for More: A soft real estate market is also often termed a buyer's market because there are typically more properties for sale than there are buyers to buy them.

This tends to drive the average sales price down often resulting in a loss for the seller.

The willingness of the seller to hold the mortgage on the property will often be compensated by a higher average sales price and through the accumulation of interest on the funds owed to the seller.

Source More Buyers: Offering creative financing options during a soft market opens up a new group of buyers who might not otherwise be home shopping.

These buyers are the ones who, for a variety of reasons, do not qualify for conventional finance methods.

These buyers will typically pay a premium pricing for a property simply for the opportunity to purchase, regardless of the conventional market conditions.

The ability to work with these additional buyers will also speed the potential sales speed because of the additional buyer base to which the seller can market.

Earn Interest: Sellers also receive the interest earnings that typically go to the banks in other transactions. These interest earnings are what make financial institutions so profitable.

Through seller financing, sellers of real estate are now able to obtain some of that profit for themselves.

The addition of interest earnings can dramatically increase the overall profit margin received from a property. Even a quick glance at an amortization schedule will show how much money is paid in interest on a yearly basis.

Each year the seller is able to hold the mortgage on their property increases the interest payments received. Often times, the seller can actually earn 50%, 100% even 150% more through the simple acceptance of interest payments.

Receive Payments: Selling a property through creative financing can provide the seller with fixed monthly payments in much the same manner as a rental property provides.

Selling a property and obtaining interest payments may actually provide a higher overall financial return than receiving rental payments for the term of ownership.

This issue is based upon the property appreciation or value retention, interest rate, amortization schedule and balloon structure negotiated.

Offset Repairs:	Through a straight sale, the seller removes the responsibility for care, upkeep, renovations, rental collections, and rental management that occur as part of a landlord's regular workday.

If something needs to be done with the property be it a general repair, regular maintenance, even upkeep such as lawn care and snow removal, it is the responsibility of the buyer not the seller to see to it that these tasks are accomplished.

This can prove financially beneficial as the expenses of the upkeep and renovations will fall on the head of the new owner rather than coming out of the landlord's pocket.

Minimize Property
Guidelines:

At times, a particular piece of real estate may not qualify for conventional financing.

If the property is in a rural location rural location the loan to value that the conventional mortgage lender is willing to lend on the property may be lower than that offered on property located in a more populated area with a higher potential buyer base.

The property may require repairs or costly renovations to qualify as collateral under the lending guidelines for the loan the potential buyers are able to receive.

> If the property is financed using a conventional loan program that requires these renovations and repairs be completed before the funding of the loan, the seller will often be responsible for seeing to it that these repairs are completed.

> The expense for these repairs will come out of the seller's pocket.

These factors and others like them make seller financing an attractive option.

> The seller is willing to hold the collateral in the current condition.

> The necessary repairs or renovations can be completed by the new owners during the period of ownership rather than by the seller before the sale.

In a private transaction, the seller may set the

sales price

terms

repair responsibility

interest rate of the loan

at any level that can be mutually agreed upon between him and the buyer.

Delay the Sale: At times, a seller will need to sell a property in a slower market.

A slow market or soft market may actually force the sales price of your home lower.

This can result in a loss to the seller.

By using creative finance options, you may be able to delay the sale of the property until the market picks up.

You may consider as an example, the lease option method of sales.

This method secures a potential buyer for the property today in the form of a tenant.

The tenant-buyer will have a vested interest in the property.

This vested interest will usually cause the buyer to treat the property in a better fashion that straight tenants often do.

This vested interest in the upkeep and care of the property provides additional security to the seller that the property will retain its value during the option period.

The use of an option period may allow the seller the opportunity to delay the final negotiation and sale of the property until the market conditions pick up.

The seller will lease the property today, collect a years worth of payments and have a potential buyer already locked in if the option is exercised by the tenant-buyer.

If the tenant-buyer chooses not to exercise their option, the sale of the property has been delayed during the lease term allowing the seller to collect monthly premiums and gain some breathing space to see if the real estate market picked up during the lease option term.

Often a year will bring about tremendous changes in the real estate market making the potential for gain by the delay a financial benefit to the seller. Lease options are explained in more depth later in the book.

As a seller, using creative finance puts you in a very powerful position to negotiate because not every seller in your market is willing to attempt these unconventional deals.

You will find you have the ability to source more buyers, more quickly, than other sellers because of the creativity you are willing to consider in your efforts to close the deal.

Creative finance sounds intimidating at first, but in reality, the processes have been in place for years. The path the buyer and seller will follow has been modified through hundreds, even thousands of transactions to create a solid base upon which you can structure your deal.

Seller financing simply means that the seller is willing to hold the paper or mortgage on a piece of real estate in a manner similar to the methods used by the banking industry.

The seller receives

- the down payment

- the monthly principal installments

- the interest for the sale of the real estate

- a higher profit than they would have with a flat sale

- the property usually sells much more quickly than if the buyers were required to obtain the purchase funds from another source

- the seller will frequently obtain additional financial benefit through

    tax breaks

    deferment of tax payments

Now, as a seller, you will have the ability to profit just as the banks always have and to sell your home in days not months!

PROFIT WITH INTEREST PAYMENTS

The interest rate that can be obtained in a creative finance scenario can truly benefit the seller. The seller can get a good selling price (or actual offer for the property) and obtain all of the monthly interest normally paid to the bank. Collecting interest is one of the primary reasons that banks are so successful and profitable. When you calculate the total of the sales price AND the monthly interest payments you will see that the actual price you obtain for the property increases dramatically.

Many buyers are interested in the bottom line - what is the monthly payment. The base monthly payment is determined by

- the loan amount

- the amortization term

- the interest rate

- if the taxes and insurance payments are to be escrowed these will also become part of the monthly payment amount

During negotiations, if you can determine the buyer's desired monthly payment you can adjust the interest rate accordingly.

- Adjusting the interest rate is often a more acceptable negotiation point to the buyer than increasing the sales price of the property.

- Many buyers look closely at their sales price and at their monthly payment.

- If these two factors fall in line with the buyer's expectations then they do not scrutinize the actual rate as closely.

Another reason to adjust the interest rate rather than the sales price is the eventual refinance the buyer's will need to obtain to cash the seller out. The refinance will be based upon the appraised value rather than the sales price and if the sales price has been inflated, the buyers will often have difficulty cashing out the seller at the agreed upon balloon term.

To see what a great benefit it is to the seller to obtain a higher interest rate, review the chart on the following pages. To create a transaction specific process, use an amortization calculator. You will quickly see that in a standard amortization, the first payments on a property are primarily applied to interest.

What this means to the seller is that they will obtain a maximum return on their investment early in the loan term.

If the seller negotiates a good balloon structure, the buyer will obtain a loan at the balloon term that has decreased very little from the initial sales price of the property.

The following chart and explanation provide more information to aid you in better understanding this point.

Principal borrowed: $102000.00
Annual Payments: 12 **Total Payments:** 360
Annual interest rate: 6.50% **Periodic interest rate:** 0.5417%
Regular Payment amount: $644.71 **Final Balloon Payment:** $0.00
Note: the following numbers are estimates. See the amortization schedule for more accurate values.
Total Repaid: $232,095.60
Total Interest Paid: $130,095.60
Interest as percentage of Principal: 127.545%

Payment	Principal	Interest	Cum Prin	Cum Int	Prin Bal
1	92.21	552.50	92.21	552.50	101907.79
2	92.71	552.00	184.92	1104.50	101815.08
3	93.21	551.50	278.13	1656.00	101721.87
4	93.72	550.99	371.85	2206.99	101628.15
5	94.22	550.49	466.07	2757.48	101533.93
6	94.73	549.98	560.80	3307.46	101439.20
7	95.25	549.46	656.05	3856.92	101343.95
8	95.76	548.95	751.81	4405.87	101248.19
9	96.28	548.43	848.09	4954.30	101151.91
10	96.80	547.91	944.89	5502.21	101055.11
11	97.33	547.38	1042.22	6049.59	100957.78
12	97.86	546.85	1140.08	6596.44	100859.92
13	98.39	546.32	1238.47	7142.76	100761.53
14	98.92	545.79	1337.39	7688.55	100662.61
15	99.45	545.26	1436.84	8233.81	100563.16
16	99.99	544.72	1536.83	8778.53	100463.17
17	100.53	544.18	1637.36	9322.71	100362.64
18	101.08	543.63	1738.44	9866.34	100261.56
19	101.63	543.08	1840.07	10409.42	100159.93
20	102.18	542.53	1942.25	10951.95	100057.75
21	102.73	541.98	2044.98	11493.93	99955.02
22	103.29	541.42	2148.27	12035.35	99851.73
23	103.85	540.86	2252.12	12576.21	99747.88
24	104.41	540.30	2356.53	13116.51	99643.47

25	104.97	539.74	2461.50	13656.25	99538.50
26	105.54	539.17	2567.04	14195.42	99432.96
27	106.11	538.60	2673.15	14734.02	99326.85
28	106.69	538.02	2779.84	15272.04	99220.16
29	107.27	537.44	2887.11	15809.48	99112.89
30	107.85	536.86	2994.96	16346.34	99005.04
31	108.43	536.28	3103.39	16882.62	98896.61
32	109.02	535.69	3212.41	17418.31	98787.59
33	109.61	535.10	3322.02	17953.41	98677.98
34	110.20	534.51	3432.22	18487.92	98567.78
35	110.80	533.91	3543.02	19021.83	98456.98
36	111.40	533.31	3654.42	19555.14	98345.58
37	112.00	532.71	3766.42	20087.85	98233.58
38	112.61	532.10	3879.03	20619.95	98120.97
39	113.22	531.49	3992.25	21151.44	98007.75
40	113.83	530.88	4106.08	21682.32	97893.92
41	114.45	530.26	4220.53	22212.58	97779.47
42	115.07	529.64	4335.60	22742.22	97664.40
43	115.69	529.02	4451.29	23271.24	97548.71
44	116.32	528.39	4567.61	23799.63	97432.39
45	116.95	527.76	4684.56	24327.39	97315.44
46	117.58	527.13	4802.14	24854.52	97197.86
47	118.22	526.49	4920.36	25381.01	97079.64
48	118.86	525.85	5039.22	25906.86	96960.78
49	119.51	525.20	5158.73	26432.06	96841.27
50	120.15	524.56	5278.88	26956.62	96721.12
51	120.80	523.91	5399.68	27480.53	96600.32
52	121.46	523.25	5521.14	28003.78	96478.86
53	122.12	522.59	5643.26	28526.37	96356.74
54	122.78	521.93	5766.04	29048.30	96233.96
55	123.44	521.27	5889.48	29569.57	96110.52
56	124.11	520.60	6013.59	30090.17	95986.41
57	124.78	519.93	6138.37	30610.10	95861.63
58	125.46	519.25	6263.83	31129.35	95736.17
59	126.14	518.57	6389.97	31647.92	95610.03
60	126.82	517.89	6516.79	32165.81	95483.21

3:1 Example Payment Breakdown

Example: The first factor to review is the total interest paid.

In this scenario, the items are amortized over a period of 30 years.

Total Repaid: $232,095.60
Total Interest Paid: $130,095.60
Actual Sales Price: $102,000.00

Consider these figures. Between principal and interest payments, the seller actually receives just over $232,000 dollars for their property!

This is an incredible amount to receive for a property whose value and sales price was only $102,000.

The one cautionary factor to consider when reviewing this schedule is that most sellers will find it a financial strain to carry a mortgage for the full 30-year term desired by most buyers.

The amortization term effects the monthly payment needed by the buyer. The buyer will often require a longer-term amortization to keep the monthly payments manageable. There is a solution which will allow the buyer to minimize the monthly payment by amortizing over the 30 year term while providing the seller with a cash-out in a timely manner.

SELLERS AND BALLOON PAYMENTS

The seller will often negotiate a balloon or cash out clause that occurs following a certain time-period or number of payments.

A balloon payment is a structure in which

The seller will accept monthly payments for a certain period of time.

After this term, the buyer will obtain funds to pay the seller in full through other means of finance.

By reviewing the chart contained in the interest section, you will see that in most amortization schedules, the early payments are applied primarily toward interest with the later payments becoming heavier on the side of principal.

In a balloon or cash-out scenario, the deal will usually be structured to amortize over a longer term.

This means that even when the buyer and seller agree that the seller will receive all of their money after five years, the loan is amortized over a 15 or 30-year term.

To amortize a sales price of $102,000 over only the five-year term would make the monthly payments very difficult for most buyers.

By amortizing over a longer term, the monthly payment is lowered to a manageable figure for the buyer.

The balloon clause ensures that the seller receives all of their funds at the five-year mark, limiting the term the seller will accept payments to a number that is reasonable from the seller's perspective.

Example: If the property sold for $102,000 and was amortized over 30 years with a balloon payment due on the 60th month the seller would receive a total of $134,165 for their property.

Sales Price + Monthly Payments of Principal and Interest = Total Cash

After the 60th payment (five years) is made, the balance owed on the property is just over $95,483.

This would be the balloon or cash out figure, or the amount the buyer must obtain from another source to cash out the seller.

In addition to this cash out or balloon payment of $95,483, the seller also must consider the monthly payments that were received during the five-year term.

The amortization schedule shows the buyers paid $644.71 monthly for 60 months.

This means that the sellers received $38,682 over the finance term.

60 payments   x $644.71   = $38,682.60

Balance at month 60 $ 95,483.21
60 months of payments $ 38,682.60
Total received by seller $134,165.81

***   When you add the cash out payment and the monthly payments the sellers have actually received just over $134,165 for their property for the simple act of "holding paper" for 60 months.

When reviewing these numbers, you can see why the negotiation of the interest rate is a very important factor to the seller. When you are in a situation where you are the one receiving interest payments a ¼ point raise in the negotiated rate can benefit you far more over the term of seller finance than a small bump in the sales price.

From the buyers perspective the ¼ point rate increase may not be as important as the final sales price. Carefully consider and review some amortization breakdowns before entering the negotiation process.

EFFECT OF AMORTIZATION TERM VS. BALLOON TERM

We have referred often to the term of finance or the amortization term versus the balloon payment. These are two very different components that are intertwined in the transaction. The amortization term will often need to be set for a longer period of time to make the monthly payments manageable for the buyer.

Using the amortization schedule shown in the interest rate section you can see that by amortizing the loan over the 30-year period the buyer's monthly payment equaled just under $645. This is a manageable payment for most people shopping the $100,000 property venue and it can be expected that if the property negotiations give the buyer a monthly payment of $645 the deal will progress smoothly.

However, most sellers do not wish to hold the mortgage paper for the full 30 years that is the amortization period required to bring the monthly payment to this level. Accepting monthly payments over this long of a term could prove a strain depending on the goals of the seller.

The seller may feel they need to remain in the area in which the property is located to protect their interest in the property. The seller may require the cash out balance for a particular goal such as college for their children or retirement. There are varieties of reasons the seller may need the money more quickly than the 30-year term.

A common solution to provide the seller with their money faster and will provide the buyer with the needed amortization term and monthly payment is to use a balloon payment clause in the negotiation. Sellers often feel that they are able to hold paper in creative finance for a certain period; we will use the example of 5 years.

The chart below illustrates how the payments would be applied if you amortized the amount financed so that the property was paid in full after five years.

The monthly payment required from the buyer would total $1995. This is an extraordinarily high payment for most buyers to attempt to manage on a monthly basis.

Principal borrowed: $102000.00
Annual Payments: 12 **Total Payments:** 61
Annual interest rate: 6.50% **Periodic interest rate:** 0.5417%
Regular Payment amount: $1995.75 **Final Balloon Payment:** $-0.19
Note: the following numbers are estimates. See the amortization schedule for more accurate values.
Total Repaid: $119744.81
Total Interest Paid: $17744.81
Interest as percentage of Principal: 17.397%

Payment	Principal	Interest	Cum Prin	Cum Int	Prin Bal
1	1443.25	552.50	1443.25	552.50	100556.75
2	1451.07	544.68	2894.32	1097.18	99105.68
3	1458.93	536.82	4353.25	1634.00	97646.75
4	1466.83	528.92	5820.08	2162.92	96179.92
5	1474.78	520.97	7294.86	2683.89	94705.14
6	1482.76	512.99	8777.62	3196.88	93222.38
7	1490.80	504.95	10268.42	3701.83	91731.58
8	1498.87	496.88	11767.29	4198.71	90232.71
9	1506.99	488.76	13274.28	4687.47	88725.72
10	1515.15	480.60	14789.43	5168.07	87210.57
11	1523.36	472.39	16312.79	5640.46	85687.21
12	1531.61	464.14	17844.40	6104.60	84155.60
13	1539.91	455.84	19384.31	6560.44	82615.69
14	1548.25	447.50	20932.56	7007.94	81067.44
15	1556.63	439.12	22489.19	7447.06	79510.81
16	1565.07	430.68	24054.26	7877.74	77945.74
17	1573.54	422.21	25627.80	8299.95	76372.20
18	1582.07	413.68	27209.87	8713.63	74790.13
19	1590.64	405.11	28800.51	9118.74	73199.49
20	1599.25	396.50	30399.76	9515.24	71600.24
21	1607.92	387.83	32007.68	9903.07	69992.32
22	1616.62	379.13	33624.30	10282.20	68375.70
23	1625.38	370.37	35249.68	10652.57	66750.32
24	1634.19	361.56	36883.87	11014.13	65116.13
25	1643.04	352.71	38526.91	11366.84	63473.09
26	1651.94	343.81	40178.85	11710.65	61821.15
27	1660.89	334.86	41839.74	12045.51	60160.26
28	1669.88	325.87	43509.62	12371.38	58490.38
29	1678.93	316.82	45188.55	12688.20	56811.45
30	1688.02	307.73	46876.57	12995.93	55123.43
31	1697.16	298.59	48573.73	13294.52	53426.27
32	1706.36	289.39	50280.09	13583.91	51719.91
33	1715.60	280.15	51995.69	13864.06	50004.31
34	1724.89	270.86	53720.58	14134.92	48279.42
35	1734.24	261.51	55454.82	14396.43	46545.18
36	1743.63	252.12	57198.45	14648.55	44801.55
37	1753.07	242.68	58951.52	14891.23	43048.48
38	1762.57	233.18	60714.09	15124.41	41285.91
39	1772.12	223.63	62486.21	15348.04	39513.79
40	1781.72	214.03	64267.93	15562.07	37732.07
41	1791.37	204.38	66059.30	15766.45	35940.70
42	1801.07	194.68	67860.37	15961.13	34139.63
43	1810.83	184.92	69671.20	16146.05	32328.80
44	1820.64	175.11	71491.84	16321.16	30508.16
45	1830.50	165.25	73322.34	16486.41	28677.66
46	1840.41	155.34	75162.75	16641.75	26837.25
47	1850.38	145.37	77013.13	16787.12	24986.87
48	1860.40	135.35	78873.53	16922.47	23126.47

49		1870.48	125.27	80744.01	17047.74	21255.99
50		1880.61	115.14	82624.62	17162.88	19375.38
51		1890.80	104.95	84515.42	17267.83	17484.58
52		1901.04	94.71	86416.46	17362.54	15583.54
53		1911.34	84.41	88327.80	17446.95	13672.20
54		1921.69	74.06	90249.49	17521.01	11750.51
55		1932.10	63.65	92181.59	17584.66	9818.41
56		1942.57	53.18	94124.16	17637.84	7875.84
57		1953.09	42.66	96077.25	17680.50	5922.75
58		1963.67	32.08	98040.92	17712.58	3959.08
59		1974.30	21.45	100015.22	17734.03	1984.78
60		1985.00	10.75	102000.22	17744.78	-0.22

3:2 Example Payment Breakdown

In order to minimize the monthly payment and bring it down to a level more manageable for the buyer, the loan could be amortized over a longer period of time than the five-year cash out request set by the seller.

> The use of a longer amortization term effectively takes care of the buyer's payment situation.

> The seller's cash out needs of receiving the lump sum of their funds at the five-year term the agreement would be met by setting a balloon or cash out from the buyer to the seller at the 5-year period.

> This option provides the seller with their money in the same time frame, as they would receive it if the loan were straight amortized over only five years.

> This method simply divides the manner of receiving the money differently.

> This different format is often more manageable for the buyer allowing for a reasonable fixed monthly payment and a certain term in which to secure other financing to pay off the seller.

This option does not provide the seller with as much money on a monthly basis but it does provide the seller with more money overall.

> If you refer to the chart above and note the accepted monthly payments of principal and interest on the sales price for 60 months, the total of all payments would be $119,744.

> This is an excellent return to the seller because they obtain the $102,000 sales price plus $17,744 in interest return.

Now, review the second amortization schedule which illustrates the figures if the seller negotiates the deal so that the amortization term is calculated over 30 years with the balloon cash out being due on the 60th month. The total of all payments for the 60 month term would equal $38,681 with the balloon payment (or balance owed at month 60) totaling an additional $95,483. When the balloon payment or cash out is received the seller actually makes $134,164 for the same property with financing over the same period.

When both amortization schedules are reviewed and the overall return over the same time frame is considered, it can be noted that a longer amortization schedule with a balloon payment benefits both the buyer and the seller.

The buyer benefits because of the lower monthly payment they will be required to make.

The seller benefits by creating an income of almost $15,000 additional money received from the property in the same time period.

The amortization and balloon terms used in the examples are just that, examples. As a seller, you will want to customize the balloon payment at the point that is best for you.

Always remember that early in the loan, most of the monthly payment is interest or pure profit for the seller. The monthly payments will often be skewered, paying more toward interest than principal, for the first 10 years of a 30-year amortization schedule. This means that a seller obtains the most profit from holding paper over the first 10 years or until the payments begin to apply toward principal more heavily than toward interest.

SALES PRICE VS. OVERALL PROFIT

Since price is typically based on value and value can vary depending on which appraiser is evaluating the property and the current market condition, you should always determine your bottom line pricing before offering a property for sale. Many considerations may affect your pricing decision.

1.   The price may vary due to an existing mortgage on the property.

Typically, the bank will not allow for a resale of the property without either paying the mortgage in full or obtaining the approval of the new buyer (assumption) from the banks underwriting department.

If you have an existing lien, it may not be sensible to sell the property for less than the mortgaged amount.

To do so would actually require additional cash out of your pocket to close the deal. There are some instances where this type of scenario may benefit you. This is an option that must be carefully considered and discussed with your bank.

2.   The price may also vary due to the condition of the property or other concessions on the part of the buyer.

In the last section, we explained the benefits of raising the interest payment received in exchange for a lower sales price on the property.

Any time a creative financing scenario is being considered, both parties should consider future plans and actions.

If the seller will need a balloon payment or cash-out within a certain time period, both parties should plan for this eventual refinance requirement.

When refinancing in the conventional mortgage market, the loan will be subject to certain factors.

> If the property needs renovations or repairs, these will often need to be completed as part of the conventional underwriting loan conditions.

> The seller will typically need to allow the buyer room to complete these renovations out of their funds prior to the required refinance.

> The completion of property repairs is often a negotiable point.

> Having the buyers complete these repairs may affect the sales price.

> If the buyer will be unable to complete the repairs before the property balloon clause requires a refinance, the seller may need to lower the sales price to allow the buyer to incorporate the costs of these renovations into the refinance loan amount. We will examine this in greater detail later in the course.

3.   Price may need to be adjusted to accommodate future refinance plans.

An important factor to consider is that all conventionally financed loans are subject to loan to value conditions.

These loan- to-value conditions are the amount the lender will be willing to finance compared to the value of the property.

The loan to value figure will vary depending on the buyer's personal situation and credit scenario.

It is important that the seller understand that at the time of refinance, the loan amount will be based upon the lower of either the sales price of the appraised value of the property.

Inflating the sales price today may severely limit the buyer's ability to refinance the mortgage in the future, especially if the property will appraise for a much lower figure.

The loan to value condition will also affect the final dollar figure the buyer can borrow.

If the buyer cannot create enough equity during the seller held finance period to meet the loan to value figures, the difference between the loan amount offered by a conventional lender and the cash out negotiated per the amortization schedule will need to be provided from another source.

These funds are usually required to be the buyer's own cash or through the securing of another mortgage or 2nd mortgage.

The eventual loan to value figure for the buyer's refinance should be carefully factored to insure a smooth transition at the time of the cash-out refinance for the seller.

Keeping the sales price fair and reasonable will aid in the eventual refinance scenario.

3. Buyers will often pay a premium pricing on a property in exchange for the option of creative finance opportunities.

    If the seller is willing to hold the mortgage for a longer term, the sales price and refinance concerns may not be an issue.

    In this case, many sellers find that in exchange for unconventional finance options a buyer will actually pay more than the value on a property.

    The primary reason a buyer will pay this extra amount above the actual value of the property is because the seller are offering creative finance options.

    The simple act of holding the mortgage on the property allows the buyer to limit the fees and points that they would be charged by a conventional lender and therefore are saving money.

    A buyer may also pay a premium price because they are being offered the opportunity obtain homeownership without the qualification process required by the bank.

    Many of the buyers who are interested in the creative finance offering are actually unable to obtain bank funding at the present time.

    This inability to qualify can occur for a variety of reasons and may or may not affect the probability that the buyer will pay the mortgage as agreed or become a factor in the negotiations.

When negotiating sales price the seller should always remember that the interest rate will also be paid into their pocket and will have a dramatic impact on the final income figures from the transaction.

Review the section concerning interest before setting a minimum acceptable sales price.

Review the section regarding interest again if you are in a negotiation where the buyer will not budge on the actual sales price but is willing to pay a higher interest rate.

Reviewing the sum total of the payments may have a large impact on the negotiation decisions.

When negotiating there will always be points that the buyer feels they are able to move and some on which the buyer takes a firm position.

When determining the deals overall appeal remember to consider all of the factors as a whole rather than taking one factor at a time and attempting to reach all of the set goals separately.

It may not make sense to kill a deal because the asking price the buyer is offering is a couple of thousand less than the sales price goal.

If the interest rate the buyer is willing to pay is 1% higher than the seller's desired level the deal may actually be more financially beneficial to the seller than the higher sales price figure the seller initially desired.

The interest rate bump may actually make the seller much more than a couple of thousand dollars over the term of the loan.

Losing the deal by pushing for that extra couple of thousand in sales price can actually cause the seller to lose long-term income if the seller forgets the potential impact of the interest rate on the final figures.

SELLING USING LEASE WITH THE OPTION TO BUY

An intelligent decision when the seller must sell and the market conditions do not meet the seller's needs would be to consider the lease with option to buy method of finance.

In this method, the buyer actually leases the property from the seller and pays an additional stipend in exchange for the right to purchase the property for agreed upon terms after a certain time period.

This option may help the seller in a variety of ways.

It allows for an additional time period (the lease period) in which the seller may pay down their existing liens to match the sales price of the property.

If carefully negotiated, the lease plus option payments may allow the seller to pay their liens using the potential buyer's funds.

A lease option allows the seller to delay the sale for the lease option term.

This delay is beneficial if the market conditions improve during that time and result in the ability to ask a higher sales price on the property than is possible today.

The option may also assist the buyers in positioning themselves for the conventional finance process ensuring the seller gains the cash out they desire.

Option payments, or the premium paid to the seller in excess of standard rent, can often be used by the buyer as a down payment when converting their mortgage to conventional finance scenarios.

The option as a down payment structure may allow the seller to sell their property to a buyer who might otherwise not have been able to save a down payment toward the purchase of a home.

If the transaction does not end in a purchase, the seller typically keeps the option stipend.

This increases the amount of money the seller receives from the home this year and allows the seller to retain that money and list the home for sell again.

The handling of the option stipend should be negotiated at the time of the signing of the lease option contract so both parties fully understand how the option stipend will be handled regardless of the outcome of the contract.

The lease with option to buy is an excellent opportunity for sellers who are currently renting a property and no longer desire the hassles and headaches that renting a property can create.

When the tenant-buyer gains a potential ownership interest in the property, they will typically care for the property in a different manner than a straight tenant.

The maintenance issues such as repair and daily activity like lawn care can be negotiated during the transaction.

The lease with the option to buy is also a good opportunity for those who must sell their property for a personal reason, for instance a job transfer during a soft real estate market.

Many sellers who must sell in a soft market are hesitant to rent their home.

They fear the property will loose value if rented because tenants sometimes do not upkeep the property in the same manner the homeowner would have done.

This lack of upkeep can result in a dramatic decrease in value leaving the seller in no better condition than if they had sold the property for a loss in a soft real estate market.

Using the lease with the option to buy method allows the seller to delay the sale of the property with a rental but obtain occupants who have a vested interest in the upkeep and value retention of the property.

This method can provide the seller with the assurance that the tenants will treat the property with more care because they may end up purchasing the property.

The lease with option to buy method also provides an additional stipend above standard market rent.

This option stipend is paid by the buyer in return for the option to purchase.

In the event the tenant chooses not to purchase the property after the option term, the seller will have this extra stipend to repair any damage that may have occurred because of the rental of the property.

The stipend should be negotiated in a fair manner that will provide enough additional security to offset the seller's risk in renting the property for the lease option term.

DOWN PAYMENT CONSIDERATIONS

The amount of the down payment is an important consideration for both the buyer and the seller. The down payment is an up-front premium the buyer must pay in a lump amount of cash. The seller must always keep in mind that one of the reasons a buyer seeks creative financing methods is that they may not have adequate funds available to meet the down payment requirements set by the lender.

- The down payment is an up-front amount of cash the seller receives. At times, the seller will need this up front payment as a source of funds for the purchase of their next property.

- The down payment also secures against default on the part of the buyer.

  A common theory in the conventional market is that the larger the amount of his or her own funds a buyer invests in the purchase of a property the less likely that buyer is to default on the loan.

This theory is a consideration for the seller since the processes for foreclosure are the same whether it is a conventionally held mortgage or a seller financed mortgage.

The seller may be more lenient concerning this condition because the seller is better able to take back the property and to re-sell the property than the bank.

A foreclosure action may actually benefit the seller since the seller will be allowed to keep all funds paid to date including down payments, lump sum payments, principal and interest.

The seller also regains the subject property, making it available for another sale that will bring the seller the full sales price opportunity.

Negotiations are a matter of knowing what you want and assessing the other party's ability to meet your needs.

Example: If you need a 5% down payment on a $100,000 house but the buyer only has ½ of that amount or $2500 available today, you may decide to negotiate a higher interest rate and request a periodic payment toward principal.

This option works well if the seller does not need the lump down payment funds up-front for their next purchase transaction. A periodic payment structure might be negotiated.

This must be customized around the information the buyer has provided during negotiations.

If the seller is aware of the fact that the buyer saved $2500 in under one year toward the purchase of the property, it might be theorized that the buyer could come up with an additional $2500 over the next year.

To capitalize on this ability to save and to meet the desired down payment figure the seller might negotiate a lump sum payment plan.

Action Plan: $2500 dollars down payment at the signing of the sales agreement

monthly payments as agreed upon based on the sales price, amortization term and interest rate

a lump sum payment toward principal of $1,000 at six months

a lump sum payment toward principal of $1,000 at 12 months

a lump sum payment toward principal of $1,000 at 18 months

This plan actually gives the seller a total down payment figure of $5500, which is more than they initially required.

The additional premium toward down payment, in this scenario $500 may be negotiated as an interest stipend to the seller in exchange for the extended payment period.

Special Note: Keep in mind that the buyer may require re-amortization at the lump sum payment dates to reflect the additional amount they have paid toward principal.

This amortization recalculation could affect the return the seller will receive through interest payments since each re-amortization lowers the principal balance on which the interest is accumulating.

Determine which is more important before negotiating additional payments toward principal a lump sum payment or increased interest earnings.

A common thought in the conventional mortgage market is that the more of their own funds a buyer has invested in a property the less likely the risk that the buyer will default on the mortgage agreement.

The down payment often becomes a sticking point in the negotiation process. If the seller wants more as a lump sum down payment and the buyer simply does not have it the deal could potentially die.

The seller will not want to lose a potentially interested buyer who is willing to meet all of the other terms desired because of a lower available down payment.

The seller could compensate for the lowered down payment by increasing the overall sales price or the interest rate.

These two factors will put more money in the seller's pocket over the term of the loan, but may enhance the risk of the buyer defaulting on the mortgage.

We have provided a scenario that might be negotiated if the buyer has excellent savings ability. If the buyer does not have excellent savings ability, there are other potential scenarios that may still be worked out.

You may want to negotiate a scenario where the missing portion of the funds the seller desires toward down payment is paid as part of the monthly payment.

What this means is dividing the missing down payment amount by the month term the seller is willing to accept and adding it to the buyers regular P&I payments.

This situation will allow the seller to recoup the desired down payment more quickly than the periodic lump sum plan but may also cause additional strain on the buyer.

The ability to negotiate based on each individuals needs, desires and ability will affect the finalized points agreed to in the transaction. The two examples provided are just that, examples. Each scenario will vary slightly and it is up to the negotiating parties to find a common ground that suits both parties.

Regardless of whether you are the buyer or the seller, when an issue arises, it is important to plan all of the possible scenarios that are acceptable to your position. Having a variety of potential scenarios available at the negotiating meeting with the other party helps find the common ground quickly and allows both parties to determine what scenario works best.

A final option for obtaining additional funds toward down payment is to allow the buyer to secure a second mortgage against the property for the purpose of down payment funds.

This mortgage would be completed at closing so the documents can be recorded immediately after the seller held mortgage at the courthouse – providing the seller with the first mortgage position.

This method will provide the seller with the up-front funds desired through the cash obtained from the second mortgage lender.

An important consideration is that the seller will not have the benefit of including the buyers own funds in the transaction as a security against default since the funds for down payment are actually a product of the secondary finance company.

This may minimize the commitment by the buyer in the transaction and so it should be carefully considered.

PROPERTY CONDITION AND FINANCE

When a buyer comes to the seller asking to buy a property using creative financing techniques, the seller must keep in mind what the property may need in order to qualify for a conventional mortgage.

The property may be in excellent condition and easily able to qualify for conventional finance

or

The property may need repairs or renovations to make it marketable and acceptable to conventional finance underwriting teams.

When a bank finances a property, there are certain minimum guidelines for property condition that must be met.

Different loan programs will require different conditions.

In some cases, the property may not qualify for conventional finance and it may not be cost-effective for the seller to perform the needed repairs and renovations.

This becomes another negotiation point.

Necessary repairs or renovations can be negotiated as part of the sales agreement in a private party transaction.

Most of the buyers in a private party transaction will be very excited about the purchase of their new home and not only willing but desirous of the opportunity to perform needed renovations.

Sometimes, the seller will find that even when they do perform extensive remodeling to the property in attempt to help the sale, the buyer will decide there are additional things or even different things that they would have done if given the opportunity. For instance, the seller may spend thousands of dollars putting in new carpeting while the buyer may have wanted the hardwood laminate flooring.

The new home is actually the buyers and in creative financing you have the opportunity to write, as a condition of sale, that the buyer is to perform the agreed-upon repairs.

The ability to require renovations or repairs to the property can benefit the seller in another way.

Any improvements to the property have the potential to increase its overall value.

The seller will have a security interest in the property and any increase in value adds to the seller's position in the event that something goes wrong over the financing term.

If a seller knows that a property has a problem, they should be up front about the situation.

Many states now require a seller's disclosure be completed for any property sold.

This seller's disclosure allows the seller to note any issues that may exist with the property.

If the seller is aware of a potential problem and fails to disclose the problem and it is later proven that the seller was aware of the issue, the seller may actually be liable for correcting the problem. There may also be other costs and penalties involved. Therefore, it is best for a seller to be honest and up front about the property.

A sample seller's disclosure is included on the following page. This is just an example to begin providing ideas to the seller of the items they may wish to disclose. You should consult a Real Estate Professional to determine what forms are applicable in your region.

SELLER'S DISCLOSURE OF PROPERTY CONDITION

CONCERNING THE PROPERTY AT: _____

THIS NOTICE IS A DISCLOSURE OF SELLER'S KNOWLEDGE OF THE CONDITION OF THE PROPERTY AS OF THE DATE SIGNED BY SELLER AND IS NOT A SUBSTITUTE FOR ANY INSPECTIONS OR WARRANTIES THE PURCHASER MAY WISH TO OBTAIN. IT IS NOT A WARRANTY OF ANY KIND BY SELLER OR SELLER'S AGENTS.

Seller _____ is _____ is not occupying the Property. If unoccupied, how long since Seller has occupied the Property?

1. The Property has the items checked below [*Write Yes (Y), No (N), or Unknown (U)*]:

____ Range	____ Oven	____ Microwave
____ Dishwasher	____ Trash Compactor	____ Disposal
____ Washer/Dryer Hookups	____ Window Screens	____ Rain Gutters
____ Security System	____ Fire Detection Equipment	____ Intercom System
____ TV Antenna	____ Cable TV Wiring	____ Satellite Dish
____ Ceiling Fan(s)	____ Attic Fan(s)	____ Exhaust Fan(s)
____ Central A/C	____ Central Heating	____ Air Conditioning
____ Plumbing System	____ Septic System	____ Public Sewer System
____ Patio/Decking	____ Outdoor Grill	____ Fences
____ Pool	____ Sauna	____ Hot Tub
____ Pool Equipment	____ Pool Heater	____ Lawn Sprinkler
____ Fireplace(s)/Chimney (Wood)	____ Fireplace(s)/Chimney	____ Gas Lines (Nat./LP)
____ Gas Fixtures Garage:	____ Attached ____ Not Attached	____ Carport
____ Garage Door Opener(s):	____ Electronic	____ Control(s)
____ Water Heater:	____ Gas	____ Electric
____ Water Supply:	____ Type: _____	
____ Roof Type: _____	Age: _____	

Are you (Seller) aware of any of the above items that are not in working condition, that have known defects, or that are in need of repair? ____Yes ____No ____Unknown. If yes, then describe.

_____
_____

2. Are you (Seller) aware of any known defects/malfunctions in any of the following? [*Write Yes (Y) if you are aware; write No (N) if you are not aware.*]

____ Interior Walls	____ Ceilings	____ Floors
____ Exterior Walls	____ Doors	____ Windows
____ Roof	____ Foundation/Slab(s)	____ Basement
____ Walls/Fences	____ Driveways	____ Sidewalks
____ Plumbing/Sewers/Septic	____ Electrical Systems	____ Lighting Fixtures
____ Other Structural Components (Describe):		

_____
_____

3:3 - Sample Seller's Disclosure Page 1 – All forms are provided for illustration purposes, you should consult with an attorney or real estate professional regarding the appropriate form for your needs.

If the answer to any of the above is yes, explain. (Attach additional sheets if necessary):

_____

_____

3.   Are you (Seller) aware of any of the following conditions? Write Yes (Y) if you are aware; write No (N) if you are not aware.

_____ Active Termites (includes

_____ Termite or Wood Rot Damage

Seller Disclosure Page 2

_____ Previous Termite Damage wood destroying insects) Needing Repair

_____ Previous Termite Treatment

_____ Previous Flooding

_____ Improper Drainage

_____ Water Penetration

_____ Located in 100-Year Floodplain

_____ Present Flood Insurance

_____ Prior Structural/Roof Repair

_____ Hazardous or Toxic Waste

_____ Asbestos Components

_____ Urea-formaldehyde Insulation

_____ Radon Gas

_____ Lead Based Paint

_____ Aluminum Wiring

_____ Previous Fires

_____ Unplatted Easements

_____ Landfill, Settling, Soil

_____ Subsurface Structure or Pits

_____ Movement, Fault Lines

If the answer to any of the above is yes, explain. (Attach additional sheets if necessary):

_____

_____

4. Are you (Seller) aware of any item, equipment, or system in or on the Property that is in need of repair? _____ Yes (if you are aware) _____ No (if you are not aware). If yes, explain (attach additional sheets as necessary).

_____

_____

5. Are you (Seller) aware of any of the following? Write Yes (Y) if you are aware; write No (N) if you are not aware.

_____ Room additions, structural modifications, or other alterations or repairs made without necessary permits or not in compliance with building codes in effect at that time.

_____ Homeowners' Association or maintenance fees or assessments.

_____ Any "common area" (facilities such as pools, tennis courts, walkways, or other areas) co-owned in undivided interest with others.

_____ Any notices of violations of deed restrictions or governmental ordinances affecting the condition or use of the Property.

_____ Any lawsuits directly or indirectly affecting the Property.

3:4 Sample Seller's Disclosure Page 2 – All forms are provided for illustration purposes, you should consult with an attorney or real estate professional regarding the appropriate form for your needs.

_____ Any condition on the Property which materially affects the physical health or safety of an
individual.

If the answer to any of the above is yes, explain. (Attach additional sheets if necessary):

_____

_____	_____
Date	Signature of Seller

The undersigned purchaser hereby acknowledges receipt of the foregoing notice.

_____	_____
Date	Signature of Purchaser

3:5 Sample Seller's Disclosure Page 3 – All forms are provided for illustration purposes, you should consult with an attorney or real estate professional regarding the appropriate form for your needs.

MINIMIZE MAINTENANCE AND RENTAL HEADACHES BY BECOMING A SELLER NOT A LANDLORD

Oftentimes sellers will be using the creative finance methods on a property that was not their primary residence. When the property did not act as the seller's primary residence, it was often a rental unit. Rental units are excellent sources of income and aid a rental property owner in building a net worth.

However property rental and property management does carry many headaches and is in effect a full-time job. By selling using the creative finance methods the seller who went into the rental property arena in attempt to capitalize on their investment, obtain a monthly payment, or even provide more stability for their family, will find that they still obtain any the same goals without the headaches and frustrations often inherent in the investment arena.

Instead of the seller performing basic maintenance functions such as snow removal and lawn care, the buyer will perform these duties as a normal part of their new home ownership activity.

When something goes wrong with a property, the seller will not receive a telephone call requesting repairs like he when he was the landlord.

The buyer, as the owner of the home, will determine the best and most cost-effective method of repairing the problem, call the service provider and take care of the problem on his own.

Creative financing allows the seller to obtain monthly payments much like they did in the rental scenario, but these are in the form of a mortgage payment rather than rent.

A property owner will often be more committed to making timely payments than a tenant because the owner has a vested interest in the property and knows that their monthly payment is building equity and stability.

A tenant is simply paying a monthly premium to keep a roof over their heads.

Selling a rental property may not appear financially beneficial at first glance.

The seller is losing many of the benefits, which first caused them to be interested in the rental property arena.

The equity growth and appreciation will now go to the buyer instead of building security for the seller.

However, reviewing the factors that that the seller receive in exchange for the sale, a seller financed sale with P&I payments will often provide more long term financial benefits than holding the rental for the same period.

The seller has the opportunity to set the sales price wherever they desire and obtain monthly payments of principal and interest, which will ultimately lead to the goal of a return on investment.

Few, if any, properties appreciate quickly enough to offset the potential interest payments a seller will receive through creative finance for the same property.

This sale versus rental units is an important factor when the landlord-seller has mastered simple and cost effective methods of property obtainment including tax sales, foreclosure properties and distressed property purchase.

If the seller has a sound source for obtaining new buildings, the use of creative financing techniques to generate a solid real estate income base through flip properties may become a full-time career.

Many retired landlords have discovered that flip property provides more long-term financial benefits and less time investment and out of pocket expense than rental units.

Even when a property is purchased for full value, the knowledge base that allows a landlord-seller to flip the property using creative finance can still provide a financial benefit.

Rental Scenario: The landlord owns:

        A single-family rental unit that is currently worth 102,000

        The landlord has the property financed at 100% loan to value with a conventional lender

        The finance carries an interest rate of 5%

The loan is amortized over 30 years

The landlord is receiving monthly rental payments of $645

The landlord is paying $547 monthly to their lender.

The landlord will earn $98.00 a month out of which he must pay:

Repairs

property taxes

Other expenses during that term

Sales Scenario: If the seller owns:

The same $102,000 property

Financed at the same terms of 100% LTV and 5% interest

Sells the property to a buyer for the same $100,000 purchase

Charges the buyer 6.5%

The seller gains a 1.5% positive cash flow income per month due to the increase interest charged to the buyer.

This positive cash flow is illustrated by the seller's 5% interest paid to their mortgage holder and the 6.5% interest paid to the seller from their seller financed buyer.

The seller receives Total interest payments over 5 years of $32,165.81 (nearly 1/3 of the mortgage)

The seller also receives $6516.79 toward the principal balance.

These two figures, rental versus sale create approximately the same income for the landlord-seller.

Rent		$	645	monthly
	x		60	months
	=		$38,700	landlord income over 5 years

Sale			
		$ 6,516.79	principal
	+	$32,165.81	interest
	=	$38,682.60	owner income over 5 years

By adding the total interest and principal received over 5 years, you can see that the funds received by both the landlord and seller are similar.

** Now what happens after the 13 years?

If the property were to be financed conventionally, the seller would still have a loan balance owed to them of $95,483.21 at the 5-year mark.

Principal + Interest Accumulations – Principal payments

That means the buyer would need to provide the seller with a lump sum figure totaling almost $95,483.21 through another method of finance in order to complete the purchase.

Assume the property was financed for 5 years and amortized over 30 years with a balloon at the fifth year.

The seller's total income for the property would be $134,165.81

		Interest Payments over 60 months	$ 32,165.81
	+	Principal Payments over 60 months	$ 6,516.71
	+	Balloon Payment due at month 60	$ 95,483.21
	=	Total to the seller	$134,165.81

This money is the seller's and the seller had none of the rental headaches, repair costs, or time investment that they would have had with a rental unit.

Plus it can be assumed that the buyer stayed in the property during the entire term so there was no need to repair and clean the property before securing new tenants, screen potential tenants or eat costs during vacancies which occur quite regularly with rental property.

Given a 12-month lease, a landlord might have had to prepare the property and invest time and energy in locating a tenant 6 times over the 6 years.

The last factor that must be considered before the profitability between the rental of an income property and the creative finance of a property is the interest payments the seller needed to make on their mortgage for the property.

The example figures give gross income for the creative finance scenario. The profitability of this type of option is dramatically affected by the seller's interest rate.

The lower the negotiated rate the seller pays as compared to the interest rate the buyer pays the higher the potential return to the seller.

This method of flipping properties holds far more profit potential if the property can be secured by the seller for a lesser price.

This method of flipping property works well for property obtained through tax sale, foreclosure or even purchasing distressed property using government funds.

The point to remember is that the sale of property using creative finance methods may prove more beneficial than the long-term rental property scenario especially when the landlord versus seller's time investment is factored as a part of the profitability assessment.

LOWER OUT-OF-POCKET COSTS FOR THE SELLER

When creative finance methods are used, the seller will oftentimes pay less out of their own pocket or out of the funds received from the transaction than they would in the conventional marketplace.

This reduction in costs often occurs for the simple reason that no real estate agent or other service providers are used in the completion of the private transaction. This is another negotiation point that may be important to the buyer because the buyer usually carries the primary expenses in the transfer of real estate.

Service providers do serve an important purpose in real estate transactions so it is best to consider whether the removal of a particular service puts you in a precarious situation.

Sometimes you will discover that certain service providers are a simple additive that, while smoothing the deal, is more costly than beneficial.

In some cases, when you are the party who has given a great deal of concession in the negotiation of other points in the transaction this may be an option to recoup some of the concessions.

There are costs the buyer or the seller typically pays in any real estate transaction, however these cost allocations are not set in stone and can be negotiated.

- If the seller concedes an interest rate point to the buyer, he may ask that the buyer pay all transfer taxes on the property.

- If the buyer pays a higher sales price, he may ask that the seller pay all inspection fees.

Who pays what is an important consideration that can benefit the party who carefully negotiates the closing cost allocations.

This option is only available when the buyers have adequate funds available or can borrow a sufficient amount to cover your down payment money, their closing costs, and the additional costs you desire them to pay.

Final Negotiation Thoughts

It is important to review every contingency outlined as well as any variations that affect your personal situation prior to the negotiation meeting. This allows you to set both minimum acceptable terms toward which you will negotiate and maximum desired goals toward which you would like the buyer to negotiate.

You will always want to set both minimum and maximum goals prior to any meeting. This allows you to compare any set of points in an offer against your minimum acceptable and maximum goals to quickly determine where you can offer concessions and what concessions you must obtain.

To illustrate the benefits behind having these guidelines fixed firmly in your mind prior to beginning negotiations, consider a scenario where:

1. You list your property for sale at $110,000 with a 7% interest rate.

2. The buyer may offer $100,000 with a 6% rate.

3. You may have determined prior to listing your property that you were willing to negotiate to $102,000 at 6 ½%.

4. This determination of the minimum acceptable offer before entering into any negotiation arena allows you to accept or decline the buyers offer quickly rather than go through the lengthy process of counter offers.

5. This early determination also allows you to negotiate the buyer's offer to your minimum acceptable price (which is what you desired in the first place) while requesting other concessions of the buyer.

   Knowing that the counter offer meets all of your minimum needs, you can then offer the buyer the pre-planned figures, appearing to have made a large concession and request concessions on other, less obvious points in exchange.

   You might ask the buyer to pay

   - all deed preparation costs

- transfer taxes

- recording fees

In many States, the transfer tax costs alone equal 2% or more of the sales price of the property.

When you view the deal as a whole, you are actually making more than your minimum acceptable price while allowing the buyer to feel they have negotiated a great deal by getting you to come down from $110,000 and 7%.

With creative finance, nearly any item on the sales agreement is open for negotiation. This is true in any real estate transaction; however, in transactions that are more conventional there are Real Estate Agents, Loan Officers, and even Underwriters taking part in the negotiation process. These added people in the process sometimes make it difficult to negotiate any factor that falls outside the norm for your area.

4

CHAPTER

The Homebuyer's and Investor Position

A buyer may choose to enter negotiations to finance a property with a private seller for a variety of reasons. The first is that one of the finest American dreams is the dream of owning a home of your own.

Fewer Guidelines:

Many people in America today are unable to secure the financing needed for the purchase of a home of their own through conventional methods.

Conventional mortgage financing relies heavily on the use of strict guidelines when determining who qualifies for a mortgage loan and the terms and conditions under which they may receive loan funds.

These guidelines are in place for a variety of reasons. Among them are statistical probability breakdowns of a potential borrower's likelihood to repay a mortgage as agreed.

Credit Issues:

There may be past or present credit issues, which cause the potential borrower to be declined by lenders.

Down payment: A borrower may have difficulty meeting the down payment requirements required by a lender under the loan programs for which they qualify.

Employment Issues: The borrower may have a history of job interruptions or unusual employment including self-employment, which place them outside the approval guidelines of lenders.

Any factor which does not fall into the normal guidelines set by the lender may disqualify a borrower for conventional financing or make the terms and condition of conventional financing very difficult for most borrowers to meet.

Added Flexibility: Seller financing provides the opportunity for flexibility. A borrower with little cash available toward a down payment may be able to negotiate with the seller to pay a higher sales price or a higher interest rate in exchange for a small amount of money down.

The same borrower may agree to pay the seller a fixed monthly amount but spread the down payment out over a period of time.

For example: the borrower may be able to pay $1,000 extra yearly toward the purchase of the home.

$1,000 down payment at the sale of the property

12 consecutive monthly mortgage payments

plus an additional $1,000 balloon payment given to the seller after one year

This process can be repeated as often as needed to obtain a satisfactory agreement between the buyer and the seller.

Conventional lenders are often not able to be as flexible in their practices as a seller.

Own Vs. Rent   Many Americans are growing tired of paying rent and desire the ability to own a home of their own and build a stable environment for themselves and their families. Seller financing provides this opportunity to more families than any other financing method available today.

Buyers are frequently surprised to discover that a monthly mortgage payment, including taxes and insurance, is equal to or even less than their monthly rental payment.

Financial Benefits: Homeowners also obtain a variety of other benefits such as tax deductions and equity growth in the home rather than simple rental payments. They will have the security of the appreciation of their asset that creates a return on the cash they invest toward their living expenses.

Control: A homeowner will even gain the ability to control their home environment making repairs, decorating and other activities a matter of choice rather than an issue that must be negotiated with the landlord.

Personal Pride: Owning a home of your own is a source of personal pride and security, which is unsurpassed through the acquisition of nearly any other possession.

These are the most prevalent reasons a buyer may choose to seek out creative finance options when purchasing a home. The following section offers further details regarding the buyer's reasons and benefits that can be obtained through creative finance.

The first and most common reasons relate to issues that affect the buyer's ability to obtain a mortgage in the conventional market place.

PAST OR PRESENT CREDIT ISSUES
AND OTHER UNDERWRITING CONDITIONS

When credit issues exist in the buyer's portfolio, either past or present, the ability to gain a conventional mortgage may be limited. When we say credit issues were not discussing only what appears on the credit report.

Other factors, which make it difficult for a buyer to obtain conventional financing, may include

o job interruptions

o unusual employment history

o past or present credit issues

o a high debt to income ratio

INTEREST, COSTS, AND CONVENTIONAL FINANCE

As a result of any of these issues, a buyer in the conventional market might have to pay much higher up-front fees and interest rate as a means of securing the loan.

Using creative finance scenario's allows the buyer to negotiate with a minimum amount of up-front closing costs and, at times, a lower interest rate than would be offered to the buyer through a conventional finance method.

Always remember creative finance scenarios are between private parties, and as long as each party receives the benefits and negotiation points, which are important to them, the situation can be customized to see the buyer's needs.

DOWNPAYMENT AND CONVENTIONAL FINANCE

At times, credit issues will also cause the lender to request additional funds be placed as a down payment toward the property.

The common theory is that the higher the amount of their own funds a buyer has invested in a transaction the lower the risk of default.

A creative seller may be willing to adjust the down payment funds to suit the buyer's current situation.

If the buyer plans to use a portion of the money they have available towards the renovation or repair of the property, this increases the seller's value and therefore the security interest, in the property.

Increased value is a benefit to the seller if the seller is actually holding the mortgage against the subject property.

The ability on the part of the buyer to perform these repairs may also allow for less out-of-pocket cash on the part of the seller prior to closing the deal.

This is a negotiation point, which should be considered when negotiating the down payment.

Creative finance sellers are often willing to assume risk that would be difficult for a lender. Lenders are not in the business of owning real estate property.

Home mortgage loans are secured against the subject real estate.

If a buyer defaults, this provides the lender with a method of securing the repayment of their monies through the sale of the property.

Banks are not set up for the ownership of real estate and the sale of foreclosed property is often a time consuming and difficult process for the bank to undertake. Therefore, the banks do try to avoid scenarios where they feel there is a higher risk of the property being returned to them.

The seller, who is financing their own real estate, does not face the same circumstances.

Regardless of the eventual outcome of the negotiated mortgage, the seller is allowed to retain all

- down payment proceeds

- monthly payments

- balloon payments

- any other funds received from the buyer.

In the event of default, the seller also receives the property.

This could mean the seller is actually able to sell the same property multiple times AND retain all of the funds from each sale.

It is less difficult for the seller to market the foreclosed property than it would be for a bank and could actually be quite financially beneficial to the seller if the buyer has made a sufficient down payment plus additional P&I payments before the property is returned to the seller.

As a buyer, your intention is to make every payment in a timely manner and avoid any foreclosure situation. However, when entering a negotiation the seller must always consider what would happen in the event of default. These factors are included not because default on the mortgage and eventual foreclosure is expected but so the buyer can understand the negotiation point or perspective of the seller.

Historically speaking, the more credit issues or unusual circumstances in a buyer's portfolio the higher the risk of default.

This is not always the case.

The buyer may know the cause of the issues that have occurred in the past and have taken steps to nullify these issues.

A bank may be unable to consider these positive steps until a certain period has passed and the results of these steps are reflected on the credit report or other documentation.

This is the primary reason many buyers seek creative financing opportunities.

The buyer should always see the negotiation of the transaction from the seller's perspective and understand that, at times, certain concessions must be granted to the seller in return for looser qualifying guidelines.

Building a higher interest rate, sales price, down payment, and other factors in exchange for the seller holding the paper on their mortgage provides incredible benefits to the buyer, even when it appears the buyer is giving on every negotiation point.

The key to successful negotiation is to assess or profile much like the seller will assess or profile, determine which negotiation points you are willing and able concede in the favor of the seller and which negotiation points are very important to the closing of the transaction from your perspective.

SMALLER DOWNPAYMENT REQUIREMENTS

Regardless of the approval level, almost every creative finance and conventional mortgage has down payment requirements that the buyer must meet.

In the conventional marketplace, these down payment funds must often be the buyer's own funds.

In other words, the down payment must not be borrowed from a friend, family member, employer or elsewhere but be from the buyer's own personal source of funds.

This stipulation is based upon the premise commonly followed in the conventional market that the higher the amount of their own funds a buyer invests in the transaction the lower the risk of default.

In creative finance scenarios, the seller will often not consider where the funds are coming from.

The seller's primary concern is often just that they received the funds.

This is another prime reason a buyer may want to enter the creative finance arena.

The ability to borrow funds, even to take a second mortgage against the property for the purpose of providing a down payment to the seller, may go a long way toward smoothing the transaction. This point alone may be the single reason the buyer is able to purchase the home today.

Creative finance scenarios will often allow the specifics of the down payment to be negotiated.

In many cases, the seller will not require the buyer to prove the source of funds.

This allows the buyer to secure the down payment as a personal loan from friends, family, employers or other sources.

Sellers may also be willing to allow the buyer to obtain a second mortgage toward the down payment of the property.

This second mortgage can often be obtained through a smaller lender or a finance company.

The second mortgage the buyer obtains will often carry a higher interest rate than the buyer may receive from the seller or would have received in the conventional market.

The buyer should remember that the interest for the second mortgage is accumulated on a smaller amount of funds.

It is also possible, in creative negotiation, to obtain a leveled down payment scenario.

Example: If the seller requires $6,000 cash down payment from the buyer and the buyer only has ½ of that amount available today, the buyer and seller may still come to an agreement.

They may close the deal now with the $3,000 down payment to be given at closing and add stipulations to the note payment documents.

Since the seller requires an overall down payment of $6,000 and the buyer only remitted $3,000 the negotiations would attempt to grant the seller the remaining $3,000 toward the needed down payment as soon as possible.

A scenario could be negotiated which allows the buyer to pay the seller $750 every six months for two years.

4 payments   x $750   = $3,000

At times, the seller may require additional compensation for the extension of the down payment period. This compensation could be negotiated as a fixed penalty or as interest added to the amount of down payment funds not paid at closing.

The options are endless and can be customized to suit the current situation of the buyer and seller.

The point to remember is that in creative finance scenarios the down payment should not stand between the buyer and the closing. As with all points in creative finance, the buyer is negotiating with an individual, and can therefore continuously work the terms and negotiation points until both parties are satisfied.

BUILD EQUITY AND SECURITY FOR YOURSELF
NOT THE LANDLORD

Many Americans are coming to realize exactly how much money they are putting into the hands of the landlord. The recent interest rate climates have caused tenants to begin comparing the costs they are paying for rent with the value of a property they could be purchasing for the same, or even less money than their monthly rental payments.

Real estate investment has created an extremely profitable arena for thousands of landlords. Today, many tenants are truly comparing the money going into the landlord's pocket monthly and returning nothing to the tenant but the roof over their heads for that month with what they could be purchasing for themselves and their family.

Tenants are becoming more financially perceptive; realizing that that same money they pay to a landlord could be providing financial security and fulfilling the dream of homeownership for the buyer and their families.

Review the principal and interest payments that are included in the seller benefits section.

When you look closely at the numbers, you will see that early in the transaction very little of the monthly payment actually goes towards the principal portion of the mortgage. However, very little is still progress. Some of the dollars do go towards the principal and eventually provide outright ownership of the home.

When you paying rent you obtain nothing in return but the fulfillment of a day-to-day obligation and you receive nothing but a day-to-day roof over your head. By actually making payments towards the purchase of the house, the buyer is building equity and security.

- With rent, every monthly payment that is made simply moves the contract closer to the end of your lease term.

- With a mortgage, every payment that is made moves the contract closer to outright ownership of the home.

BUILD SECURITY FOR THE FUTURE

More and more people are concerned with how they will survive their retirement years.

Building equity in a home can provide financial stability for the future.

A mortgage can be paid off and therefore there will be no housing payments during the time when you no longer earn a regulated income.

A homeowner builds equity in the home with each payment. This equity can then be sold providing a large lump sum upon which to live during their retirement.

A homebuyer can even purchase today, build equity and then sell the home and invest those funds in a more expensive and larger house.

These are considerations not negotiation points. These are factors that the buyers must consider as a simple benefit of homeownership regardless of the specific terms of finance negotiated.

Most people do not rent for the convenience of renting.

Most people rent because they believe they cannot own homes of their own. In many Instances, that is true.

Using creative financing techniques provides the option of homeownership to more buyers than ever before.

When negotiating the terms of your creative finance mortgage, you should always keep in the back of your mind the fact that the benefits provided through simple ownership will sometimes outweigh the negotiation points that do not finalize in your favor. These points might be ones in which you should concede to the seller because you will still be building equity and security through this new mortgage.

FULFILL THE AMERICAN DREAM

Homeownership, pride and respect!

Have you ever dreamed about sitting around the barbecue with your family and friends on the weekend?

Have you wished you could show off the new renovations and beautiful stylized decor you have completed on your home?

This is the American Dream. Owning a home of your own.

It is difficult to have that barbecue in a little apartment. Even when you live in a large complex, you have to fend off the neighbors each time you use the public areas for a gathering.

Landlords tend to make apartment decor durable and generic.

This allows the landlord to save expenses each time the tenancy of his unit changes.

Each of us has a different personality and we want our homes to reflect that personality.

KENNEY

- Can you do that in the apartment you rent today?

- What about expansion and renovations?

- Can you remodel your home to suit your needs?

- Or that pet you would love to have?

- Does your landlord agree that that darling puppy or cute kitty would make an excellent addition to your household?

These are just some of the many and very basic, day-to-day considerations that make obtaining a home of your own are the dream of so many Americans.

Creative finance offers more people, who today must comply with every rule and regulation set by their landlord, the opportunity to take charge and begin making decisions of their own!

People who own their homes have taken more control of their lives.

They come home after long days work, pull into the driveway, walk in the front door and realize that the home, the driveway, the door, all they see belongs to them!

This is a tremendous source of personal pride for many Americans and the foremost goal of many more.

Have you ever been filling out a form or application and been asked

"do you own or rent?"

Or even

"is there an apartment number?"

Do you somehow feel less when you must answer YES! I rent!

The sense of pride you will feel and the respect you will achieve as a homeowner makes pursuing the purchase of a home, regardless of the type of finance that must be obtained, well worth the efforts you must put forth.

EQUITY GROWTH, APPRECIATION AND FINANCIAL GAIN

Most people approach the decision to buy a home for emotional reasons. They know they desire, want and need a home of their own. However, there are many financial benefits inherent in the simple ownership of a home of your own.

These financial considerations can dramatically impact your life.

These financial benefits are in place whether you use conventional finance or creative finance techniques to purchase your home.

These benefits include equity growth, appreciation and a return on cash investment.

Renting a property provides none of these benefits.

Equity: The amount of ownership interest one has in the property occurs when the amount owed for the property is less than the amount the property is worth.

Every payment that is made towards the principal mortgage amount of the property increases the equity position in a property.

If you purchase a property today, that is

valued at	$100,000
finance the full offer price of	$100,000
principal payments made	$ 2,000

you have a 2 percent ownership interest or equity position in the property

$100,000 Financed
$ 2,000 Principal Paid in 1 year
        2% equity position gained through payments

Now you own a home that is valued at $100,000 and you only owe $98,000.

Over the years, this equity position grows, providing a financial basis upon which to plan the rest of your life. This provides additional security for your retirement years or for other reasons.

Once you own your home, you can often secure an additional loan against the equity available in your property for other events in life that would otherwise present a great financial strain.

The birth of a child

That child's education

Starting a business

The potential reasons are endless and will be different for every buyer but through homeownership, attaining those dreams becomes a little bit easier.

Appreciation:

In addition to the equity growth you generate by making payments, real estate undergoes another profitable process. Appreciation is the increase in the value of an object. Economic conditions, regional variances, and inflation can all affect the value of your home. Real estate is one purchase that regularly appreciates in value.

In the years after World War II, many Americans purchased their home for as little as $2,000 or $4,000.

These same homes are now worth $50,000, $70,000, or more.

This is an incredible return on the buyer's investment.

This return required no action on the part of the buyer; it simply occurred as a result of natural appreciation.

It is unlikely that property will appreciate as quickly over the coming years, but any form of appreciation is money gained through passive activity.

One secret of the wealthy is passive income.

Active income requires your time and efforts.

Passive income is gained simply by virtue of the deals that can be negotiated.

Tax Benefits:

There are varieties of tax benefits you can obtain through homeownership.

One benefit is the ability to deduct all or a portion of your interest payments. You should review your potential tax benefits with an accountant to determine exactly how owning a home of your own can best benefit you.

The financial benefits of homeownership are wide and varied. The ones mentioned here are only the most common. Consider your personal situation and the benefits you may obtain from purchasing a home of your own to determine additional ways creative finance solutions can truly benefit you.

LOWER CLOSING COSTS

Buyers are often shocked when they first see their good-faith estimate in the conventional mortgage market.

There are many costs involved in the closing of a home loan.

Most of these costs are paid to service providers who are vital to the transaction and to the security interests of the buyer.

Some of these costs might be avoided in a creative finance transaction.

Creative finance transaction are completed between the buyer and the seller or privately.

That means that there is no loan officer structuring the deal and no bank lending the money.

Generally, removing the loan officer and the lender from the transaction can save the buyer 1 percent, 2 percent even up to 10 percent if they have credit issues in their profile.

These savings are the fees or payments that would have been paid to the loan officer as payment for their services in helping the buyer obtain the loan.

These costs are fair because the loan officer does work hard negotiating, structuring and securing the financing.

The same funds that were used to pay the loan officer and other service providers in the mortgage transaction during a conventional process can be used in creative financing for other very important items.

These funds may be used to

- repair the property

- provide extra down payment security for the seller

- stay in the buyer's bank account to provide additional financial stability following the new home purchase

Some of the benefits highlighted in this chapter are simply benefits, which the buyer will receive from purchasing a home of their own regardless of the financing method utilized.

The benefits of homeownership will be different for every buyer and are virtually endless. Any benefit is based upon the buyer's specific situation. Other benefits are based on the use of creative finance techniques.

What every buyer needs to understand is that there are basic benefits and additional benefits within each negotiation point, benefits that are inherent to the transaction.

The ability to own your own home is perhaps the single most important factor in the creative finance arena.

You should also remember that the method of payment and the terms negotiated could have a dramatic impact on the financial benefits received from the transaction.

There will be points on which you may give and points on which you will want to stand firm. These will be based upon your needs and your plans for the property and so will be different for each buyer. Some of the items that will be negotiated by you and the seller are listed in the next section. This list is for illustrative purposes and is designed to provide you with a general outline to be customized to suit your particular situation.

PRICE VS. RATE

Sometimes, the only factor a buyer considers is the sales price. The sales price is the base amount you, as the buyer will pay for a particular property. Sales price is an important consideration but is not the only factor to be considered.

The following amortization chart which shows the total payments made if the sales price is set at 102,000 with 6.5% interest and amortized over 30 years.

Principal borrowed: $102000.00
Annual Payments: 12 **Total Payments:** 361
Annual interest rate: 6.50% **Periodic interest rate:** 0.5417%
Regular Payment amount: $644.71 **Final Balloon Payment:** $-0.68
Note: the following numbers are estimates. See the amortization schedule for more accurate values.
Total Repaid: $232094.92
Total Interest Paid: $130094.92
Interest as percentage of Principal: 127.544%

Payment	Principal	Interest	Cum Prin	Cum Int	Prin Bal
1	92.21	552.50	92.21	552.50	101907.79
2	92.71	552.00	184.92	1104.50	101815.08
3	93.21	551.50	278.13	1656.00	101721.87
4	93.72	550.99	371.85	2206.99	101628.15
5	94.22	550.49	466.07	2757.48	101533.93
6	94.73	549.98	560.80	3307.46	101439.20
7	95.25	549.46	656.05	3856.92	101343.95
8	95.76	548.95	751.81	4405.87	101248.19
9	96.28	548.43	848.09	4954.30	101151.91
10	96.80	547.91	944.89	5502.21	101055.11
11	97.33	547.38	1042.22	6049.59	100957.78
12	97.86	546.85	1140.08	6596.44	100859.92
13	98.39	546.32	1238.47	7142.76	100761.53
14	98.92	545.79	1337.39	7688.55	100662.61
15	99.45	545.26	1436.84	8233.81	100563.16
16	99.99	544.72	1536.83	8778.53	100463.17
17	100.53	544.18	1637.36	9322.71	100362.64
18	101.08	543.63	1738.44	9866.34	100261.56
19	101.63	543.08	1840.07	10409.42	100159.93
20	102.18	542.53	1942.25	10951.95	100057.75
21	102.73	541.98	2044.98	11493.93	99955.02
22	103.29	541.42	2148.27	12035.35	99851.73
23	103.85	540.86	2252.12	12576.21	99747.88
24	104.41	540.30	2356.53	13116.51	99643.47
25	104.97	539.74	2461.50	13656.25	99538.50
26	105.54	539.17	2567.04	14195.42	99432.96
27	106.11	538.60	2673.15	14734.02	99326.85
28	106.69	538.02	2779.84	15272.04	99220.16
29	107.27	537.44	2887.11	15809.48	99112.89
30	107.85	536.86	2994.96	16346.34	99005.04
31	108.43	536.28	3103.39	16882.62	98896.61
32	109.02	535.69	3212.41	17418.31	98787.59
33	109.61	535.10	3322.02	17953.41	98677.98
34	110.20	534.51	3432.22	18487.92	98567.78
35	110.80	533.91	3543.02	19021.83	98456.98
36	111.40	533.31	3654.42	19555.14	98345.58
37	112.00	532.71	3766.42	20087.85	98233.58
38	112.61	532.10	3879.03	20619.95	98120.97
39	113.22	531.49	3992.25	21151.44	98007.75
40	113.83	530.88	4106.08	21682.32	97893.92
41	114.45	530.26	4220.53	22212.58	97779.47
42	115.07	529.64	4335.60	22742.22	97664.40
43	115.69	529.02	4451.29	23271.24	97548.71
44	116.32	528.39	4567.61	23799.63	97432.39
45	116.95	527.76	4684.56	24327.39	97315.44
46	117.58	527.13	4802.14	24854.52	97197.86
47	118.22	526.49	4920.36	25381.01	97079.64
48	118.86	525.85	5039.22	25906.86	96960.78

49	119.51	525.20	5158.73	26432.06	96841.27
50	120.15	524.56	5278.88	26956.62	96721.12
51	120.80	523.91	5399.68	27480.53	96600.32
52	121.46	523.25	5521.14	28003.78	96478.86
53	122.12	522.59	5643.26	28526.37	96356.74
54	122.78	521.93	5766.04	29048.30	96233.96
55	123.44	521.27	5889.48	29569.57	96110.52
56	124.11	520.60	6013.59	30090.17	95986.41
57	124.78	519.93	6138.37	30610.10	95861.63
58	125.46	519.25	6263.83	31129.35	95736.17
59	126.14	518.57	6389.97	31647.92	95610.03
60	126.82	517.89	6516.79	32165.81	95483.21

4:1 Example Payment Breakdown

As you can see, over the first 60 months you would pay approximately $38,682 dollars.

The cash out or amount owed on that $102,000 mortgage after 60 months is $95,483.

If you pay off that balance at the 60th month, you would actually have ended up paying $134,165 for the property.

Now, if you negotiated the sales price to $105,000, which means you would be paying "more" for the property, but lower the interest rate by 1% and review the chart again you will see the potential change to your spending.

Principal borrowed: $105000.00
Annual Payments: 12 Total Payments: 361
Annual interest rate: 5.50% Periodic interest rate: 0.4583%
Regular Payment amount: $596.18 Final Balloon Payment: $-1.41
Note: the following numbers are estimates. See the amortization schedule for more accurate values.
Total Repaid: $214623.39
Total Interest Paid: $109623.39
Interest as percentage of Principal: 104.403%

Payment	Principal	Interest	Cum Prin	Cum Int	Prin Bal
1	114.93	481.25	114.93	481.25	104885.07
2	115.46	480.72	230.39	961.97	104769.61
3	115.99	480.19	346.38	1442.16	104653.62
4	116.52	479.66	462.90	1921.82	104537.10
5	117.05	479.13	579.95	2400.95	104420.05
6	117.59	478.59	697.54	2879.54	104302.46
7	118.13	478.05	815.67	3357.59	104184.33
8	118.67	477.51	934.34	3835.10	104065.66
9	119.21	476.97	1053.55	4312.07	103946.45
10	119.76	476.42	1173.31	4788.49	103826.69
11	120.31	475.87	1293.62	5264.36	103706.38
12	120.86	475.32	1414.48	5739.68	103585.52

13	121.41	474.77	1535.89	6214.45	103464.11
14	121.97	474.21	1657.86	6688.66	103342.14
15	122.53	473.65	1780.39	7162.31	103219.61
16	123.09	473.09	1903.48	7635.40	103096.52
17	123.65	472.53	2027.13	8107.93	102972.87
18	124.22	471.96	2151.35	8579.89	102848.65
19	124.79	471.39	2276.14	9051.28	102723.86
20	125.36	470.82	2401.50	9522.10	102598.50
21	125.94	470.24	2527.44	9992.34	102472.56
22	126.51	469.67	2653.95	10462.01	102346.05
23	127.09	469.09	2781.04	10931.10	102218.96
24	127.68	468.50	2908.72	11399.60	102091.28
25	128.26	467.92	3036.98	11867.52	101963.02
26	128.85	467.33	3165.83	12334.85	101834.17
27	129.44	466.74	3295.27	12801.59	101704.73
28	130.03	466.15	3425.30	13267.74	101574.70
29	130.63	465.55	3555.93	13733.29	101444.07
30	131.23	464.95	3687.16	14198.24	101312.84
31	131.83	464.35	3818.99	14662.59	101181.01
32	132.43	463.75	3951.42	15126.34	101048.58
33	133.04	463.14	4084.46	15589.48	100915.54
34	133.65	462.53	4218.11	16052.01	100781.89
35	134.26	461.92	4352.37	16513.93	100647.63
36	134.88	461.30	4487.25	16975.23	100512.75
37	135.50	460.68	4622.75	17435.91	100377.25
38	136.12	460.06	4758.87	17895.97	100241.13
39	136.74	459.44	4895.61	18355.41	100104.39
40	137.37	458.81	5032.98	18814.22	99967.02
41	138.00	458.18	5170.98	19272.40	99829.02
42	138.63	457.55	5309.61	19729.95	99690.39
43	139.27	456.91	5448.88	20186.86	99551.12
44	139.90	456.28	5588.78	20643.14	99411.22
45	140.55	455.63	5729.33	21098.77	99270.67
46	141.19	454.99	5870.52	21553.76	99129.48
47	141.84	454.34	6012.36	22008.10	98987.64
48	142.49	453.69	6154.85	22461.79	98845.15
49	143.14	453.04	6297.99	22914.83	98702.01
50	143.80	452.38	6441.79	23367.21	98558.21
51	144.45	451.73	6586.24	23818.94	98413.76
52	145.12	451.06	6731.36	24270.00	98268.64
53	145.78	450.40	6877.14	24720.40	98122.86
54	146.45	449.73	7023.59	25170.13	97976.41
55	147.12	449.06	7170.71	25619.19	97829.29
56	147.80	448.38	7318.51	26067.57	97681.49
57	148.47	447.71	7466.98	26515.28	97533.02
58	149.15	447.03	7616.13	26962.31	97383.87
59	149.84	446.34	7765.97	27408.65	97234.03
60	150.52	445.66	7916.49	27854.31	97083.51

4:2 Example Payment Breakdown

As you can see, lowering the interest rate but offering a higher sales price would save you approximately 2,000 dollars over the five-year term.

You can work the numbers in a variety of ways to determine which point of negotiation is best for you but always attempt to negotiate the points which are most beneficial to you.

If you offer a higher than the asking sales price, the seller will typically be willing to offer some concessions in other areas.

A concession on the interest rate may save you more over the life of the loan than a concession on any other point.

The desire for an interest rate concession will depend on you plans.

If you intend to make the required monthly payments to the seller for the offered term and refinance the mortgage in the conventional market after that term, the interest rate may not make that much difference to you in the long run.

However, there will be times that you will want to pay a higher interest rate in an effort to secure the home.

If you are aware that you can refinance into a conventional mortgage with an excellent rate in only 12 months it may benefit you to offer the seller a much higher interest rate for the finance term but a lower sales price.

The other negotiation points should remain the same (amortization term and balloon payment.)

> The longer the amortization terms the lower your required monthly payment.

> This does not mean that you cannot make additional payments toward principal; it simply means that you only have to make the minimum payment as negotiated.

In addition, keeping the balloon term at 60 months, as shown in the examples, provides you with breathing room in the event the refinance does not occur in the time frame planned.

If you offer the seller a higher interest rate in exchange for a lower sales price, you will actually have the opportunity to show immediate equity in the property.

Equity is a very important consideration when applying for a conventional mortgage.

The conventional lender will want you to have a certain amount of vested interest in the property.

The theory is that the larger your equity position in the property (either in the form of paper equity, the value compared to the amount owed or in the form of a cash down payment out of your own pocket) the lower the risk of default.

By paying a slightly higher interest rate to the seller during the term of creative finance you are spending a bit more for the seller finance term on a monthly basis, but you will be asking for a lower sales price in exchange.

This lower sales price provides immediate equity value, which will enable you to refinance without a large amount of cash out of your pocket.

Example: At the refinance, the conventional lender requires a 90% LTV position meaning the lender will finance 90% of the value and you must provide 10% of the value as either equity or down payment money.

Using the $102,000 property we used for the examples earlier, if you plan to refinance after 1 year you would have paid the seller monthly payments totaling $7,736 and still owe a balance of $100,859.

In order to refinance at a 90% LTV you would obtain a loan of $91,800 and need to have equity and cash down money totaling $10,200.

If you make monthly payments for the 12-month term at the 6.5% interest used in the charts, you would have paid only $1,141 toward principal.

You would need to make a cash down payment out of your pocket of $9,059 to qualify for the conventional refinance loan.

Payment	Principal	Interest	Cum Prin	Cum Int	Prin Bal
1	92.21	552.50	92.21	552.50	101907.79
2	92.71	552.00	184.92	1104.50	101815.08
3	93.21	551.50	278.13	1656.00	101721.87
4	93.72	550.99	371.85	2206.99	101628.15
5	94.22	550.49	466.07	2757.48	101533.93
6	94.73	549.98	560.80	3307.46	101439.20
7	95.25	549.46	656.05	3856.92	101343.95
8	95.76	548.95	751.81	4405.87	101248.19
9	96.28	548.43	848.09	4954.30	101151.91
10	96.80	547.91	944.89	5502.21	101055.11
11	97.33	547.38	1042.22	6049.59	100957.78
12	97.86	546.85	1140.08	6596.44	100859.92

4:4 Example Payment Breakdown

Example #2:   If you offered the seller 8.5% interest and a sales price of $92,000 the seller sees that they have the potential to obtain a much higher return over the life of the loan. You may have to use an amortization schedule to illustrate this potential gain to the seller. The seller would accumulating up to $162,600 worth of interest over the life of the loan as opposed to $110,000 they would have obtained if you offered the higher sales price and the lower interest rate. In negotiation, you are not under any obligation to explain your future refinance plans to the seller.

Given the lower sales price and higher interest rate, you will make slightly higher payments during the term of finance with the seller, but have a much stronger equity position from the first day of purchase.

Using this scenario, the house would still be worth $102, 000 but at the 12th month, you would owe $91,304.
Using the same lender requirement of 10% equity position or down payment, the lender would still be willing to finance (or provide a loan amount) of up to $91,800.

This scenario allows you have a lower payoff balance owed to the seller than the lender is willing to provide in a loan. This means no down payments will be needed out of your pocket.

Principal borrowed: $92000.00
Annual Payments: 12 **Total Payments:** 361
Annual interest rate: 8.50% **Periodic interest rate:** 0.7083%
Regular Payment amount: $707.40 **Final Balloon Payment:** $0.67
Note: the following numbers are estimates. See the amortization schedule for more accurate values.
Total Repaid: $254664.67
Total Interest Paid: $162664.67
Interest as percentage of Principal: 176.809%

Payment	Principal	Interest	Cum Prin	Cum Int	Prin Bal
1	55.73	651.67	55.73	651.67	91944.27
2	56.13	651.27	111.86	1302.94	91888.14
3	56.53	650.87	168.39	1953.81	91831.61
4	56.93	650.47	225.32	2604.28	91774.68
5	57.33	650.07	282.65	3254.35	91717.35
6	57.74	649.66	340.39	3904.01	91659.61
7	58.14	649.26	398.53	4553.27	91601.47
8	58.56	648.84	457.09	5202.11	91542.91
9	58.97	648.43	516.06	5850.54	91483.94
10	59.39	648.01	575.45	6498.55	91424.55
11	59.81	647.59	635.26	7146.14	91364.74
12	60.23	647.17	695.49	7793.31	91304.51

4:5 Example Payment Breakdown

Each scenario is different and you should experiment with a variety of amortization schedules and speak with the conventional lenders in your area to determine what the qualification requirements will be for a refinance. Sometimes it is not beneficial to refinance early in the transaction, but at other times, it will work in your favor.

Regardless of your goals, knowing what you plan to do in the near future will enable you to negotiate the transaction today putting you in a more favorable position in the long term. If you plan to stay in the seller held mortgage for the entire balloon term, a lower rate against a higher sales price may prove more beneficial because it may provide you a lower monthly payment. If you plan to refinance quickly, the lower sales price with a higher interest rate may prove more beneficial to you because it allows for a higher equity position from the first day of ownership.

ABILTY TO MAKE ADDITIONAL PRINCIPAL PAYMENTS
Equity as an investment plan

Another factor to consider is that early in the transaction you are paying the most interest.

In actuality, the bulk of your monthly payment will be applied toward interest for the first 10 years of the loan term.

While this is a negative in some ways, most mortgages are structured this way.

A possible method of offsetting some of the interest accumulation is to be certain you are allowed to make additional payments towards principal.

By making only 1 extra payment per year toward principal, you actually make 5 extra payments in the first five years.

This allows you to save approximately $2,300 in interest if the loan is re-amortized to reflect the additional payment at the 12th month of each year.

These extra payments toward principal would total almost $3,225, saving you a total over the five years of $5,525 dollars.

additional principal paid   +   interest accumulation saved

This is a consideration most buyers fail to note. If you can come up with just one extra payment per year, you may actually reduce your overall costs by a great deal over the life of the loan.

When negotiating the loan terms it is important to be certain that there are no clauses against making additional payments toward principal and that the seller will re-amortize at least once per payment year to reflect the additional principal payments.

AMORITIZATION TERM AND BALLOON PAYMENTS

For the buyer, the bottom line often boils down to the monthly payment.

This factor is affected by the amortization term.

This does not always mean how long the seller is willing to hold the mortgage but rather how long they are willing to factor the payments.

You can request any amortization term you desire, but promise a cash out or balloon payment at a particular point so the seller still receives their money in the same period.

If the seller requires all of their money in only five years, you would need to pay almost $2,000 dollars monthly under a straight amortization schedule.

This figure is calculated based on a sales price of $102,000 and an interest rate of 6.5 percent if the loan was amortized over only 5 years.

This is not a manageable monthly payment for most people.

The other option is to negotiate a scenario where the seller amortizes the mortgage over 30 years, bringing your payment down to $645 monthly.

This payment is calculated at the same $102,000 sales price and 6.5% interest rate but with a longer amortization term.

To receive this amortization term and still provide the seller with all of the funds within the requested five-year term, you would offer the seller a balloon payment cash out after five years.

This balloon payment, cash out provides the seller with the balance owed toward the sales price at a fixed time. This will often satisfy the sellers need to obtain the cash in a timely manner while lowering your monthly outgo.

5

CHAPTER

The Real Estate Agent

Real Estate Sales is a competitive business where your reputation for negotiating and closing deals is essential to continued success. The integration of creative finance into your transaction repertoire can dramatically increase your ability to source buyers, negotiate sales and conduct a specialized form of transaction negotiation that many of your competition simply does not understand. These factors will increase your reputation within your market making you the Agent with whom every buyer and seller wants to work.

Sell more/Earn More:

A Realtor who takes the time to learn and fully understand creative finance methodology will find that they are dramatically increasing their business and income potential.

There are many more buyers out there who desire a home of their own than are being sourced by the real estate agents in your area.

These buyers may be unable to qualify for conventional financing for any of the negotiating reasons that we have outlined on the previous pages or a variety of other reasons.

> This does not make them bad buyers this just means to get them into home you must be creative.

Statistics have shown that up to 40 percent of buyers have difficulty obtaining conventional financing.

By offering these buyers the opportunity to purchase one of your listings or even another agents listing through creative finance methods, you actually gain the ability to increase your business AND income by 40% this year.

In fact, the numbers may actually higher than 40% because for each buyer there must be a seller.

If you have a seller who may be open to the creative finance options, you stand the chance of increasing your business twice.

> Once (40%) by finding a buyer who otherwise would not have actually bought a property and earning the seller agent commission and again (40%) by selling your own listing that might not otherwise have sold before the listing term expired.

Sell more listings:

In addition to finding more buyers to put together with open-minded sellers there may be properties in your listing files that simply have not sold because the property requires repairs renovations that make it difficult to obtain financing on the property.

Conventional mortgage programs often require that the property being financed meet certain levels or standards.

Example: the government rural housing loan requires a certain amount of insulation be built into the property

FHA requires a certain amount of energy efficiency be a part of the property.

If your listing does not meet the guidelines set by underwriting, the property cannot be closed or may only close with conditions.

The guidelines will often require that these deficiencies be corrected prior to closing or require enough funds be credited at closings so the required corrections can be completed in a timely manner.

Factors such as these can cause listings in your files to sit unsold until the listings actually expire, losing you money.

By showing the seller the potential benefits of creative finance techniques, you may be actually able to close on these properties today.

You will allow the new buyers to perform the much-needed and required repairs so that the property will qualify for conventional financing in the future.

Simply adding a thorough understanding of creative finance technique and an open-mindedness to use these techniques when needed, you may actually build an entire business base or expand a current successful Realtor business.

If you assess the statistics of properties that do not sell and potential buyers who are lost because they do not qualify for a home mortgage, you will see that there is a potential to actually double your closed deals.

Sell faster:

Real estate agents will find their listings actually sell much more quickly if creative finance techniques are advertised.

> Advertising creative financing does not mean that every listing that offers creative finance options will sell using creative finance techniques.

> Advertising creative finance options simply means that more buyers that are interested will call – up to 40% more!

This is an advertising technique to help stimulate interest in your property listings.

You may actually find other agents will show your property more often, therefore becoming familiar with the property.

> The more familiar other agents are with your listings the more likely they will be to recommend it to other buyers.

Be certain to get the agreement of the seller to consider creative finance options before using this advertising tool.

Build Stronger
Referral Systems:

You actually have the opportunity to expand the pipeline of your referring mortgage lending partners as well.

Many loan officers miss a very important loophole in the underwriting guidelines.

Just because a buyer qualifies for 97% loan to value does not mean that buyer must take the 97% loan to value.

> Most underwriting guidelines require that the difference between the Loan and the Sales Price be the borrower's own funds.

> This particular stipulation causes many loans to fall apart before the ever get to the closing table.

The loophole written into many guidelines is that if the loan taken by the buyer is much lower than the maximum approval loan to value the money may not need to be to be sourced as the borrower's own funds.

Example: If the borrower is approved for a 97% loan to value and accepts an 80% loan to value, the underwriting guidelines often state that source of the additional 20% need not be proven or be the borrower's own funds.

> This 20% can then take the form of a seller held second mortgage.

This provides the perfect opportunity to close more deals, to sell the home faster for your sellers and for your cash poor buyers to obtain a home today.

Your loan officer partners will benefit because they are able to close more deals.

Granted the loan amounts will be lower but the deals will close.

In effect, the loan officer writes the first mortgage for 80% of the sales price of the property, which effectively removes the underwriting guidelines for sourcing down payment because the amount borrowed is far lower than the maximum approval.

You help negotiate a seller held second mortgage on the property.

The seller will finance 20% of the sales price of the property as a second mortgage.

This allows the sellers to receive a lump sum 80% of the sales price, monthly payments on 20% of the sales price plus any interest that can be negotiated on that second mortgage.

You might also want to discuss seller concession toward closing costs with both your lending partner and the seller. By offering a seller concession, you may be able to conduct a transaction where the buyer does not need to bring any money to close!

Carefully review the accumulation of interest section of this book for more information on how holding a mortgage, even if it is only a second mortgage, can provide more money to your seller.

The ability to negotiate a first and second mortgage for your buyers will dramatically decrease the time frame needed to sell your properties.

This practice will make you a very popular real estate agent in your market and the creative methods you use will generate customer referrals as well as lending partner referrals, because you will be one of the few Agents who truly understand this type of opportunity.

6

CHAPTER

Negotiating Terms and Conditions

Once you understand the benefits and potential risk factors for each party involved in the creative financing transaction as well as the types of deals commonly negotiated, you are ready to begin the process of negotiation.

The process of negotiation boils down to two essential actions

- negotiating the actual terms and conditions for your creative finance scenario

- selling the other party on these terms and conditions

All real estate transactions contain many of the same key components such as a buyer, a seller, and a piece of property. Each real estate transaction will also contain components specific to that particular transaction and the needs of the parties involved.

- You would not charge a tremendous monthly payment to a buyer who is unable to afford it because that would raise the potential for issues in the future.

- You may want to offer a higher sales price or interest rate to a seller who is willing to bend on the down payment or other terms to ensure they leave the table satisfied.

In the following pages, we will discuss negotiation points.

Negotiation is a matter of determining your minimum desired factors and working your way to an agreement that meets these requirements.

In other words, you may concede on an unimportant factor from your perspective but is an important factor to the other party.

In exchange for this concession, you will try to gain their agreement to a factor that is vital in your mind but may not seem as important to the other party. Negotiation is a give and take scenario.

To succeed at negotiation you must ensure you give on points that will not hinder you while taking on points that will benefit you the most.

The art of negotiation is a very complex discussion. Some people have an innate ability to negotiate well while others do not. Regardless of your skill level, you should be able to negotiate your sale in a competent manner that is satisfactory to both parties.

The first step in negotiation is to plan a strategy.

To plan a strategy you must determine the minimum guidelines to the deal that are acceptable to you.

This does not mean that your deal will only obtain the minimum you desire for each factor.

Understanding your minimum guidelines before the negotiation meeting allows you to establish your negotiation position so that you can competently negotiate those factors that are important to you while making what will appear to be concessions to the other party.

If you do not know the minimum acceptable levels to which you are willing to negotiate, you cannot quickly ascertain that your negotiation points are still above these levels.

Any negotiation will require concessions toward the other party's goals.

These concessions will be factors which are not as important to you or whose minimum acceptable levels are met by the maximum acceptable levels of the other party.

The seller will be looking for agreements that meet and EXCEED their minimum acceptable levels.

The buyers will be looking for agreements or points which meet or ARE LOWER than their maximum acceptable levels.

Example: A buyer sees a property listed as "Article Considered" with the advertisement stating the following:

> Sales Price $110,000
> Interest 7%
> 10% down payment

This listing contains the maximum goals of the seller.

> This is the "best case" scenarios, which the seller does not necessarily believe he will receive but will consistently negotiate towards.

> Any concession the seller receives towards this maximum desired level enhances the deal for the seller.

A buyer who would like this property may decide before negotiations begin that the best-case scenario for them would be:

> Sales Price $100,000
> Interest 6%
> Down payment 5%

> This is the minimum acceptable level toward which the buyer will want to negotiate.

As you can see, the seller and the buyer are very far apart in the initial look at the deal.

However, both parties should also have factored where they are willing to negotiate in other words their minimum necessary requirements.

If the seller has determined prior to the listing their minimum acceptable parameters which include:

> Sales Price $102,000
> Interest 6 ½ %
> Down payment 5%

You can see that the deal is much closer to being a successful negotiation.

These figures signify the lowest possible levels the seller is willing to accept.

Any offer from the buyer that does not meet these minimum guidelines can be quickly discounted or countered.

The seller can quickly assess an offer to see that all of the points offered by the buyer do surpass his minimum requirements.

This allows the seller to accept the deal immediately or even negotiate to exceed the minimum offer, bringing the deal closer to the seller's maximum parameters.

When looking at the seller's minimum guidelines you will note that the buyer's initial offer and the seller's minimum acceptable level still do not meet. The next step is to determine the buyer's maximum parameters, or the most the buyer has determined they are able or willing to pay.

In the example above the buyers maximum acceptable points were:

Sales Price $105,000
Interest rate: 6 ½%
Down payment: 5%.

If you carefully review all four sets of numbers,

The seller's minimum acceptable negotiation or worst case

Sales Price $102,000
Interest 6 ½ %
Down payment 5%

The seller's maximum acceptable negotiation or best case

Sales Price $110,000
Interest 7%
10% down payment

The buyer's minimum acceptable negotiation or best case

Sales Price $100,000
Interest 6%
Down payment 5%

The buyer's maximum acceptable negotiation or worst case

Sales Price $105,000
Interest rate: 6 ½%
Down payment: 5%.

you will see that the deal is an actual workable option for both parties.

While the initial asking price and the buyer's best-case scenario were rather far apart, the seller's minimum requirements and the buyers maximum requirements actually overlap on the three key points each has determined are important to them.

With open negotiations, this deal went to closing and both parties walked away happy feeling that the deal was a good one for them.

The key to successful negotiations is to determine

- what benefits you wish to obtain from the transaction

- solidify your desires (starting negotiation factors)

- outline your needs (where you will negotiate to close the deal)

After you have determined what you want and what you need or the lowest you are willing to accept you are halfway prepared for the negotiation section.

The second half of the preparation is to attempt to gauge what is important to the other party. If you can determine what benefits they receive from each negotiation point, you will be able to highlight the benefit to them while in fact, be negotiating toward your desired levels.

COMMONLY NEGOTIATED POINTS

Deed handling: The handling of the deed is one of the simplest points to negotiate but it can have a dramatic impact on how secure each party feels about the transaction. There are a variety of deed handling options that have been used in the past. Each of these options was popularized for a particular reason and may be a workable option in your transaction.

1.   The deed can be transferred and recorded upon the fulfillment of the terms of the sales agreement.

This is a straight handling and follows much the same practices as a conventional finance transaction.

An offer is made that is eventually accepted by both parties.

Any conditions written into the sales agreement such as inspections are completed.

The transaction proceeds to a closing where the deed is witnessed and then recorded at the county recorder's offices.

The payments are then made until the mortgage, which was recorded against the deed, is paid in full.

At the time the final payments are made the mortgage and note are satisfied at the recorder's office and the deed that was recorded is then the buyer's free and clear providing no other obligations have been incurred during the note term which effect the deed.

2.   The deed may be held in escrow until such time as the transaction has reached completion and all conditions have been fulfilled and then recorded.

This method is commonly termed a contract for deed.

The sales agreement is negotiated and all conditions of the sales agreement are met.

The deed is prepared for the closing but in this case, it is not recorded.

At the closing the deed is signed and witnessed but then is given to a third party, typically a real estate professional or attorney.

This third party holds the deed until all terms of the purchase have been met.

In this scenario, the note and mortgage may or may not be recorded at the county recorder's office.

This is based on the negotiation between the parties.

Upon the receipt by the seller of the last of the purchase monies and the confirmation that all purchase conditions have been met, the third party records the mortgage under the buyer's name at the courthouse.

4. The deed creation can be delayed until such time as the transaction has been finalized with all purchase conditions and payments have been completed.

This scenario may also be termed a contract for deed but it is the most private of the deed handling methods.

This process allows for the seller to retain the deed in its entirety until all conditions of the sale have been met.

At the time of the last payment or satisfaction of the last condition, the seller signs the deed with witnesses and then records the paperwork at the county recorder's office.

Each option in the handling of the deed provides different feelings of security to the parties involved in the transaction.

This is an excellent point to bring up at the negotiation table because it is often not considered.

By bringing this issue to the surface, either party is then able to concede a point concerning the handling of the deed and perhaps obtain a benefit of another point in exchange.

Down payment: The seller will often look for the highest possible down payment while the buyer will often look for the lowest down payment they can obtain.

The seller wants a higher down payment because the down money provides an immediate lump sum amount in their pocket and helps secure the buyers performance.

It is commonly believed in the conventional market that the higher the amount of money invested out of the buyer's pocket, the less chance the buyer will default.

In a scenario where the buyer has invested only a small amount out of their own pocket in the property, the amount lost if the buyers choose to default is minimal.

The buyer will often negotiate for the least amount of down money possible.

Putting less money down often allows the buyer to retain that cash for other purposes such as repairs or remodeling of the property, the purchase of furniture and home decor items for their new home or even as a savings buffer to aid them in making the monthly mortgage payments or yearly tax and insurance payments.

There are various reasons a buyer may negotiate hard on the down payment requirements.

One of the most important is that the buyer may simply not have the money available to meet the seller's desired down payments.

At the beginning of most negotiations, the down payment is a point where the buyer and seller initially appear to be rather far apart in their desired requirements. The deal may still be negotiated to both parties' satisfaction.

The seller may simply negotiate other terms and conditions, which are of a benefit to them while conceding to the buyer's desire for lower down payment.

If a lower down payment is one of the only firm needs the buyer has set the seller may be able to obtain all of the other terms they find desirable in exchange for this one concession.

This ability should be carefully considered since obtaining agreement on all other points in the process could be more financially beneficial to the seller over the term of the agreement.

Conversely, the seller may unwilling or unable to accept the lower down payment.

If the seller is unwilling or unable to accept the down payment being offered, even when all other points in the negotiation are set in the seller's favor, there are other options that may be considered.

Lump Sum Payment:

A lump sum payment agreement schedule may be put into place.

A lump sum agreement schedule calls for the buyer to make lump sum payments to the seller at designated time periods over the term of the mortgage.

For instance if the seller requires $5,000 down payment and the buyer has 80% of this figure or $4,000 available at the time of the signing of the sales agreement, the seller may require the buyer make additional payments towards the deficit at designated times.

> The seller might negotiate the deal so that the buyer makes a $1000 balloon payment after one year of ownership.

> The seller might also divide the amount owed and write the agreement so they receive periodic payments toward the down payment deficit.

> The agreement may state that the buyer must pay an additional $100 monthly to the seller to offset down payment requirements.

> It is important to note an additional negotiation point, which may come into play when a lump sum down payment is added to the conditions of the sale.

The amortization of the lump sum payments should be negotiated.

Whenever a buyer makes a payment toward the principal amount owed, the interest accumulations are effected.

The method or re-amortization and the time that this amortization occurs can dramatically affect the interest the seller is receiving and the amount the buyer owes.

Another factor to consider when negotiating the down payment is condition of the property at the time of the sale.

The seller may accept a smaller down payment in exchange for the buyer's agreement to perform necessary repairs or renovations to the property.

> The seller should always remember that any repairs or renovations performed by the buyer to the property increase the overall value of the property.

> In addition to buyer's performance of the repair is means that the money for those repairs does not come out of pocket of the seller.

> This benefits the buyer because they may not need to spend the money as one lump sum, as they would with a down payment.

It is important to negotiate a time frame for the repairs, which will meet the buyer's expenditure schedule while allowing the repairs to be completed in a timely manner.

The seller may wish to negotiate an inspection clause that allows them to assess the completion and professionalism of the repairs.

This negotiation point can often be obtained by pointing out that the seller is providing a concession by allowing the buyer to complete these repairs.

This is a desirable point because the seller will want to ensure there is no loss in value to the collateral.

The buyer may also minimize the total amount required out of their pocket by paying a higher down payment figure but require the seller perform these repairs.

This point allows for less overall expenses out of the pocket of the buyer because the seller will spend the funds to repair or renovate the property.

The funds that are spent are often paid out of the buyer's down payment and so are, in effect, the same monies.

The point to remember is that if the repairs end up going over budget the additional costs will be carried by the seller.

The important point concerning down payment is that while it seems very important at the time of the initial negotiations, over the term of the creative finance scenario the down payment may actually be only a small portion of the overall money exchanged.

Monthly Payment: Monthly payments are often a very important factor to the buyer.

The monthly payment is, in most cases, the buyer's bottom line.

The buyer will often be willing to negotiate on the

sales price

interest payments

repairs renovations

other factors that are important to the seller

if the seller is able to structure the deal so that the buyer's monthly payment requirements are met

The seller will typically desire the highest possible monthly payment they can gain. However, the seller should also review how much of the monthly payments received are credited only toward interest versus principal.

An important factor that many sellers fail to consider is that early in the loan process monthly payments are credited almost entirely towards the interest payment in most amortization schedules.

What this means to the seller is regardless of the amount of money the buyer pays to them monthly, the funds credited only toward interest are profit for the seller.

These payments have very little effect on the principal loan balance allowing the seller to retain almost the full value of the cash out at the balloon term.

This option allows the seller to negotiate the monthly payment to a level that is acceptable to the buyer and fits their budget while obtaining an incredible recovery through the receipt of interest heavy payments.

Interest Rate: Interest payments are one of the most important factors that have made creative financing programs popular from the seller's perspective.

The ability to gain interest is what has made banks so very profitable and now the sellers are able to obtain some of this profit for themselves.

Amortization schedules will affect exactly how much interest the seller receives, as will be exact interest percentage and the balloon term.

The sections concerning amortization schedules should be carefully reviewed by the seller to see just what impact the interest rate will have on the transaction.

At times, the seller can actually double the amount they receive from the property through the simple acceptance of monthly interest payments.

The intelligent seller will structure the transaction so that they accept the payments on a monthly basis that apply most heavily to the interest rate with very little effect on the principal balance.

The same seller will then structure the balloon schedule to occur at the time that the monthly payments become heavier on the side of principal.

This allows the seller to obtain income through monthly payments and still maintain a cash out balance similar to the initial sales price negotiated.

That means that all of the monthly payments obtained by the seller are nearly 100% profit.

Interest rate is also a very important factor to the buyer.

As illustrated by the charts included in the sections concerning interest rate the amount of interest paid on a loan actually increases the overall cost of property to the buyer, often by a large amount of money.

The buyer should remember that no matter how one finances the property, creatively or conventionally, they would pay interest.

It will benefit the buyer to research the current interest rate climate in the conventional marketplace prior to beginning the negotiation of the interest rate with the seller.

The buyer should also remember that the seller is assuming risk by creatively financing the mortgage.

The buyer will want to carefully reviewed the current interest rate in the conventional marketplace, and consider the maximum interest rate they are willing to pay to the seller in return for the creative finance concessions they are receiving.

Interest can accumulate very quickly but amortization term may be a more important factor to the buyer than the interest paid over the term. The illustrations included in the earlier sections under interest rate show a property that sold for $102,000. In this particular instance, the seller wanted the complete cash or balloon payment of the loan balance after five years but agreed to amortize the monthly payments and interest over 30 years. This extended amortization term served to lower the monthly payment expected from the buyer.

The balloon term allows the seller to obtain their funds in a timely manner while providing enough time for the buyer to accomplish certain tasks in preparation for the conventional refinance or cash out to the seller.

The seller finance term should be used by the buyer to

reposition their personal credit profile

save the additional funds required by the conventional marketplace to close a home loan

put additional money into the property allowing it to qualify for conventional finance

The ability to obtain the property while accomplishing these tasks should be a primary consideration in the buyer's mind when considering how much interest they are willing to pay.

The buyer should always compare the total interest they will pay at various rates during the negotiations to determine the actual costs incurred by raising the interest rate.

These costs must then be compared to the benefits the buyer is receiving through seller finance to determine if the money spent is worth the benefits received.

Interest is going to be a very important factor to the seller. It is important for the buyer to understand exactly what the seller receives from the interest rate.

The buyer must determine the maximum they willing to pay the seller overall and compare it to what they will pay in interest.

It is often an easy sale to show the seller benefits of the higher interest rate or even the benefits of the ability to collect interest as part of your negotiation process.

It is also important to remember that many sellers who are willing to hold creative finance paper have not read this course or another course like it.

The purpose of this course is allow you to understand the positioning of the other party and to provide you with the information you need to adequately negotiate the points that are important to you while selling the benefits to the other party.

Sales Price: Sales price is another important consideration to both the seller and the buyer.

The buyer must remember that the sales price listed on the sales agreement may have no bearing when compared to what is actually paid for the property over the life of loan.

> The amortization schedules shown earlier illustrate what is actually paid for the property.
>
> When principal and interest payments are accumulated over the thirty-year life of a loan the actual amount spent varies a great deal from the initial cost of the property.
>
> It may benefit the buyer and seller to negotiate a higher sales price.

The buyer should carefully consider the sales price compared to the interest payments that will be made on the property over the life of the loan to determine which scenario works best for their particular situation.

Both parties will also want to keep in mind the refinance period as negotiated by the sales agreement.

> If, at the time of refinance, the buyer has obtained little or no equity in the property the conventional underwriter may require a large lump sum out of the buyer's pocket as security against the loan.
>
> This lump sum goes toward the down payment or equity position of the buyer.
>
> If the sales price is negotiated at the time of the initial sale to be much lower than the value of the property, the buyer will have built in equity from the first day.
>
> This built in equity may make the transition to a conventional mortgage at the time of the balloon cash-out period an easier process for the buyer.

Both the buyer and the seller should also review current market values for the same type of property.

If, at the time of the refinance transaction the property does not appraise for enough to cover the sales price, alternate methods of making up the difference will be required.

Regardless of the buyer's credit profile and approval level, most conventional finance loans will base the loan amount on the lower of the Sales Price or Appraised Value.

If the property sale is negotiated above market value, the property might not appraise for the correct figure at the time of the refinance transaction. This might inhibit or stop the refinance option creating issues for both parties.

Example: Sales Price $ 100,000
                  Appraised Value $ 90,000

If the LTV approval is set at 97% LTV, the loan amount will be based on the Appraised Value:

                  Appraised Value $ 90,000
                  LTV   x   97%
                  Loan Amount $ 87,300

It will be difficult for the borrower to generate $12,700 in equity over the term of creative finance unless the term for cash-out is set well into the future.

The difference between the loan amount and what is owed to the seller will need to be obtained from other sources.

> If the buyer is unable to gain the necessary funds to make up the difference between the Loan Amount offered in conventional finance and the amount owed to the seller the seller may be forced to accept less money than previously negotiated or even foreclose on the property.

This information should be carefully considered as the need for conventional finance may make it more beneficial to offer a lower sales price and a much higher interest rate to the seller in exchange for the simple benefit of obtaining equity for the refinance.

When we discuss negotiation points, we explain that the purpose of a negotiation point is to find a common meeting point between what is important to you and what is important to the other party.

Each person's negotiation point goals will be different because the parties involved in the process will be different and have a variety of goals and personal situations.

The negotiation points discussed are meant to provide a starting point for consideration.

You will want to expand upon these points and carefully review the sales agreements commonly used to determine what other points you may wish to include in your negotiations

Escrows: The handling of taxes and homeowner's insurance premiums is another very important factor to both parties.

The seller may choose to require the buyer make a certain premium payment monthly on top of their principal and interest payments toward the yearly homeowner's insurance premiums and property tax bills.

This monthly premium will be held in a reserve account. This reserve account allows the funds required paying these bills to be available when the bills come due.

The transaction may also be structured so that the buyer makes yearly premium payments towards homeowner's insurance and property taxes as they come due.

This allows the buyer to manage their funds on their own throughout the year and make payments as needed.

The important factor, for both parties, is to ensure that these bills are paid in a timely manner. Anytime these payments are not made, the position of both parties is in jeopardy. Regardless of the method of payment negotiated, both parties will want to double check to ensure that these payments are being paid as agreed.

Partial Finance: At times, the seller may be unable to hold the entire mortgage against the property.

This may be due to the sellers need

to pay off an existing lien or mortgage

to use the proceeds from this transaction to purchase their next deal

or for other financial reasons.

Oftentimes a buyer will be able to qualify for a conventional mortgage if the seller is willing to hold a certain percentage of the sales price of the property as a second mortgage.

It was explained earlier that many loan guidelines have a loophole or qualifying criteria that states if the loan-to-value ratio is below a certain percentage none of the funds towards the closing of the transaction must be sourced.

> The second mortgage will need to be completed and recorded in tandem with the closing of the conventional mortgage so that the paper trail is clear for the underwriter's file.

> What this means is that if the seller holds that stipulated percentage, the difference between the loan-to-value and the sales price, the loan can proceed without any verification of the funds used for the purchase.

> This lack of verification of funds towards closing will often allow a buyer who otherwise would not have been able to obtain the conventional finance to get the mortgage.

> This provides the cash out to the seller in the form of a bank loan.

This is actually the best of both worlds for the seller.

> They obtain a large lump sum cash out in the form of the first mortgage.

> They also are able to obtain interest and principal payments on a monthly basis.

> > The ability to obtain interest payments increases the overall value the seller receives from the property.

Always remember to discuss this possibility with the loan officer with whom the buyer chooses to work.

The transaction will need to be structured based on the advice of the loan officer, in order to comply with underwriting guidelines.

Amortization and
Balloon payments: Amortization and Balloon payments factor in any creative finance transaction.

> The length of time the loan is amortized will dramatically affect the buyer's monthly payment.
>
> The amortization term also affects the amount of interest received by the seller.
>
> Amortization term need not affect the time that the seller actually holds the mortgage.
>
> Amortization term simply affects the length of time those payments are factored.

Earlier we showed how the amortization schedule could dramatically affect the amount of interest that is accumulated and the amount of the monthly payment that is credited towards interest or pure profit for the seller. Given that factor, the longer amortization term is actually more profitable for the seller than a shorter amortization term.

> The dollar figure of the monthly payment will be lower, but the amount of that monthly payment is credited more toward interest than principal.

The longer amortization term also benefits the buyer because their monthly payments will be much lower than with a shorter amortization term.

> The ability of most buyers to pay off a $100,000 mortgage in five years is very limited; however, most buyers shopping the $100,000 price range can afford a monthly payment on $100,000 if the payment is amortized over 30 years.
>
> From the buyer's perspective they are making very little progress toward paying the principal balance of the loan, however they are limiting their monthly payment to a more manageable level.

The use of a balloon payment is what allows the seller to obtain the cash they need within the period the desire.

Balloon payments can be set at any term that is agreeable to the buyer and seller.

An easy way to determine the balloon term is to discuss with a conventional loan officer the buyer's ability to qualify if they follow certain guideline tactics.

Many loan officers will be able to review buyer's current scenario and give them specific requirements, which must be met in order to qualify for conventional finance.

Discuss the balloon term with the buyer's loan officer or perspective loan officer and then sent a level that is comfortable for both the buyer in the seller.

The seller may want to provide the buyer with an additional amount of time in the balloon term beyond what is recommended by the loan officer.

This provides the buyer the opportunity to correct any other issues, which may arise in the buyer's attempt to follow the guidelines set forth by the lender.

You also want to ensure that the balloon term meets the sellers need for a cash out of the balance of the loan.

Sellers also want to consider the amount of interest that they receive in the monthly payments within the balloon term.

Over the first ten years of a typical amortization term, the bulk of the monthly payment is allocated towards interest.

Because interest is profit for the seller, the seller will want to determine how long they can afford to carry the mortgage, and compare that term against when the mortgage loses profitability.

Lease-Option: Negotiating a lease with an option to buy is a very different scenario from other creative finance options.

A lease with an option to buy is simply a lease in which the potential buyer pays an additional monthly stipend to gain the right to be the first person allowed to buy a particular piece of property.

When negotiating a lease with an option to buy the terms of potential sale is typically negotiated at the time of the signing of the lease agreement.

This up-front negotiation allows the buyer to understand what they will be paying for the property and to determine the feasibility of a final purchase during the term of the lease.

Stipend: The monthly stipend given to the seller is typically granted simply for the right to be the first to purchase the property.

The handling of the stipend must be negotiated at the time of the initial lease contract. In other words, if the perspective buyer chooses not to exercise their option does the seller retain the monthly stipend that was paid or is it refunded to the buyer.

If the buyer chooses to exercise the option

> is that monthly stipend simply an extra amount that was granted to the seller?

> is that monthly stipend an amount the seller is willing to allocate as part of the down payment on the property?

> > In other words, will the stipend be credited toward the sales price of the property?

These are important factors to consider and put into writing from the first negotiation to avoid confusion later in the lease term.

When a lease option is being negotiated, the buyer should also speak with a lending professional to determine what requirements will be in place to use the option stipend paid toward the eventual purchase loan obtained for that property.

Closing Costs: The payment of closing costs is often another important factor to negotiate in creative financing.

Closing costs can have a large impact on the overall amount of money needed at the closing of the transaction.

Closing cost will vary depending on the service providers the buyer and seller choose to use.

In conventional finance, there are closing costs that are customarily paid by the buyer or the seller, however creative finance allows for complete negotiation.

The decision concerning the payments of closing costs in one that is open for negotiation.

Some closing costs may even be delayed until a later point in the transaction.

Example: the transfer taxes must be paid at the time the mortgage, deed, and note are recorded at the county recorder office.

If the transaction were written as a contract for deed with none of the documents being placed on file until the purchase money has been fully paid, the transfer taxes would be delayed until that recording date.

This allows the seller the opportunity to obtain additional funds.

Example: if the buyer was unable to meet the seller's desired down payment, the seller may negotiate the contract so the buyer pays the transfer taxes at the time the property is transferred.

This delays the need for the buyer to have the required funds until later in the transaction but provides the seller with additional funds.

Transfer taxes can be more than 2 percent of the sales price of the property.

The agreement that the buyer would pay the transfer taxes at the time the mortgage and note are recorded may actually increase the amount of money that the seller technically receives.

The allocation of closing costs also affects the overall price or sales price the seller receives. Oftentimes the seller's closing costs are paid out of the amount of money the seller receives at the closing table. The ability of the seller to gain the agreement from the buyer to pay these costs means less money out of the sales price and therefore affects the seller's net of the closing table.

Property Condition: A buyer and seller should also always keep in mind the condition of the property. An essential issue is what needs to be done with the property when negotiating the sale.

This is an important factor when a buyer attempts to obtain conventional financing. In order to pass underwriting a property must meet certain minimum guidelines.

The condition of a particular property and the cost of the repairs and renovations needed are a common reason many sellers choose to offer creative finance solutions.

If the property is financed under a conventional loan program, the seller may have to pay the costs of these repairs or renovations. These repairs do not typically increase the property value enough to offset the costs.

A common negotiation point in creative financing is to give the buyer a break on the down payment or the sales price for the property in exchange for they buyer's agreement to perform the needed repair by a certain date.

This agreement gives the seller an increase in the value of the property.

Since the seller is holding that property as security against the amount the buyer owes this is typically a benefit.

In addition, the cost of these repairs and renovations comes out of the buyer's funds allowing the seller to retain the profits from the sale for themselves.

One factor to keep in mind is that unless the buyer is a professional contractor or has a good understanding of the work involved the parties may want to put into the contract that all work must be inspected by a licensed professional.

It is also a good idea to write a clause that the buyer is responsible for following local inspection and permit laws.

Using creative financing with a property that needs renovations or repairs allows the property to transfer ownership today.

The new owner-buyer's are able to perform the repairs in their own time.

The repaired property may then qualify for conventional finance.

	Minimum Acceptable Goals	Maximum Desired Goals	Offer #1	Counter-Offer	Offer #2	Counter-Offer	Final Decisions
Sales Price							
Interest Rate							
Monthly Payment							
Down Payment							
Additional Down Payment							
Closing Costs Buyer Paid							
Closing Costs Seller Paid							
Deed Handling							
Amortization Term							
Balloon Payment							
Repairs - Buyer							
Repairs – Seller							
Seller 2nd at Refinance							

6:1 Sample Form – Negotiation Elements

The items included are examples only. Each transaction will vary and the goals of each party in the transaction will vary. You should customize the form to include the items that are important to both you and the other party in the transaction. The items included are for example purposes only and should not be considered the final authority on the points that should enter your personal negotiations.

Understanding Contracts

Before you begin actual negotiations, you must have a general understanding of the contracts and documents that you will be using. The material included in this section will provide you with the basic components of these documents. When completing the actual agreements and contracts it is a good idea to retain the services of a competent attorney or real estate professional.

A contract is a legally enforceable agreement, which states a party will or will not do a certain thing.

Contracts need not be lengthy or difficult, but they must meet certain requirements to be legally binding.

A contract may either be an expressed contract, which is when both parties to the contract declare their intentions either in writing or orally or through an implied contract.

Expressed Contract   A lease agreement or a sales agreement qualifies as an expressed contract.

The landlord or seller expresses their intent to lease or sell a property to the tenant or buyer.

The tenant or buyer expresses their intent to make rental or purchase money payments to the landlord or seller.

Real estate contracts must be in writing and in most states must contain some monetary exchange to be valid.

The monetary exchange can be as little as $1.00 but funds must transfer between the parties.

Implied Contract   An implied contract is created by the actions of the involved parties. These types of contracts are not typically used in a real estate transaction.

An implied contract is not expressed in writing but rather results from actions, which indicate intent to do something.

For example ordering dinner in a restaurant implies the intent to pay for the foods and services received.

To be valid a contract must meet all of the requirements of the law. A contract that meets all the requirements of the law is termed legally binding and is enforceable in a court of law.

For a contract to be legally valid, it must be executed between legally competent parties.

Competency is determined by a variety of standards, which can be termed either objective or subjective.

Competency requirements state that the person entering the contract must be of legal age to enter into such a contract and the person must not be intoxicated or under the influence of mind-altering substances when the contract is negotiated.

This particular requirement is subject to interpretation.

People who have been declared incompetent by a judge may not make a valid contract.

The contract must contain points, which are mutually agreed upon by both parties, and the points must be lawful.

The contract is granted for consideration or cause, in other words for payment of good or valuable consideration or the receipt of a service.

In some instances the contract must be executed in writing, the law governing the particular type of contract you are attempting to execute determines this factor.

If the conditions creating a valid contract are met, any party to the contract may enforce the terms of the contract in a court of law.

A standard Agreement for the sale of real estate is available for purchase at many stationary stores or even real estate offices. You may also retain the services of an attorney for the preparation of your sales agreement and other documents needed for the transaction. The standard form will guide you through a formal and legal offer for the sale of real estate and the acceptance of the offer.

When working with properties that will be sold and financed outside of the normal process, you will either need to create addenda to the Sales Agreement or have a real estate professional create a sales agreement customized to the details of your transaction. These addenda or additional contracts will be customized to fit the circumstances of sale or custom design a sales agreement for use with your particular transaction.

You may purchase a standard sales agreement from stationary stores, real estate offices or from an attorney who specializes in real estate transactions. The following pages will guide you through the components of a standard agreement for the sale of real estate as well as various addenda that you may encounter in your transaction. Your real estate professional or competent attorney will assist you in determining the correct documents for use in your particular transaction but a thorough understanding of the contracts and documents used will assist you in ensuring your transaction meets all of your needs.

REAL ESTATE PURCHASE CONTRACT

STATE OF _____

COUNTY OF _____

1. PARTIES: _____

(Hereinafter known as Seller) agrees to sell and convey to _____

_____ (Hereinafter known as Purchaser), and Purchaser agrees to buy from Seller the Property described below.

2. PROPERTY: (a)Address: _____

_____(insert full address) specifically described as

_____

_____

_____, or as described in the attached exhibit.

(b) *Improvements:* The house, garage and all other fixtures and improvements attached to the above-described real property, including without limitation, the following permanently installed and built-in items, if any: all equipment and appliances, valances, screens, shutters, awnings, wall-to-wall carpeting, mirrors, ceiling fans, attic fans, mail boxes, television antennas and satellite dish system and equipment, heating and air-conditioning units, security

---

7:1 Example Form – Real Estate Sales Contract – Private

and fire detection equipment, wiring, plumbing and lighting fixtures, chandeliers, water softener system, kitchen equipment, garage door openers, cleaning equipment, shrubbery, landscaping, outdoor cooking equipment, and all other property owned by Seller and attached to the above described real property.

(c) *Accessories:* The following described related accessories, if any: window air conditioning units, stove, fireplace screens, curtains and rods, blinds, window shades, draperies and rods, controls for satellite dish system, controls for garage door openers, entry gate controls, door keys, mailbox keys, above ground pool, swimming pool equipment and maintenance accessories, and artificial fireplace logs. (d) *Exclusions:* The following improvements and accessories will be retained by Seller and excluded:_____

_____

The land, improvements and accessories are collectively referred to as the "Property".

3. **PURCHASE PRICE:** The Total Price shall be $_____ payable as follows:

Earnest money: (Receipt of which is hereby acknowledged)	$_____
Cash or certified funds due at closing:	$_____
Finance Instrument to be held by Seller _____	$_____

4. **FINANCING:** The portion of Sales Price not payable in cash will be paid as follows:

(a) *Third Party Financing:* One or more third party mortgage loans in the total amount of $_____. If the Property does not satisfy the lenders' underwriting requirements for the loan(s), this contract will terminate and the earnest money will be refunded to Purchaser.

(b) This contract is subject to Purchaser being approved for the financing described in the attached *Third Party Financing Condition Addendum.*

(c) This contract is not subject to Purchaser being approved for financing and does not involve FHA or VA financing.

(d) *Assumption:* The assumption of the unpaid principal balance of one or more promissory notes described in the attached *Loan Assumption Addendum.*

(c) *Seller Financing:* A promissory note from Purchaser to Seller of $_____ bearing _____% interest per annum, secured by _____ mortgage, or _____ vendor's and deed of trust liens, and containing the terms and conditions described in the attached *Seller Financing Addendum.* If an owner policy of title insurance is furnished, Purchaser shall furnish Seller with a mortgagee policy of title insurance.

5. **TITLE INSURANCE:** Seller agrees to furnish to Purchaser a standard form title insurance commitment, issued by a company qualified to insure titles in _____, in the amount of the purchase price, insuring the mortgagee against loss on account of any defect or encumbrance in the title, unless herein excepted; otherwise, the earnest money shall be refunded. Said property is sold and is to be conveyed subject to any mineral and mining rights not owned by the undersigned Seller and subject to present zoning classification.

7:1 Example Form – Real Estate Sales Contract – Private Continued

6. **PRORATIONS & HAZARD INSURANCE:** The taxes, as determined on the date of closing, are to be prorated between Seller and Purchaser as of the date of delivery of the deed. Seller shall keep in force sufficient hazard insurance on the property to protect all interests until this sale is closed and the deed delivered. If the property is destroyed or materially damaged between the date hereof and the closing and Seller is unable or unwilling to restore it to its previous condition prior to closing, Purchaser shall have the option of canceling the contract and receiving back the earnest money, or accepting the property in its damaged condition, any insurance proceeds otherwise payable to Seller by reason of such damage shall be applied to the balance of the purchase price or otherwise be payable to Purchaser.

7. **CLOSING COSTS & DATE:** The sale shall be closed and the deed delivered within sixty (60) days from the execution of this Agreement by all parties, except Seller shall have a reasonable length of time within which to perfect title or cure defects in the title to the said property. The Seller agrees to pay the cost of deed preparation and a mortgagee's title insurance policy, all other closing costs shall be paid by Purchaser. Purchaser agrees to allow Seller to remain in possession of said property subject to separate terms of a month-to-month lease agreement to be executed at closing for a lease period not to extend beyond

_____.

8. **CONVEYANCE:** Seller agrees to convey a good merchantable title and General Warranty Deed of said property insuring that property is free of all encumbrances, except as hereinabove set out and Seller and Purchaser agree that any encumbrances shall be paid in full at the time of closing from sales proceeds.

9. **CONDITION OF PROPERTY:**
   (a) *General Provisions and Obligations of Parties:* Seller agrees to deliver the heating, cooling, plumbing, and electrical systems and any built-in appliances in operable condition at the time of closing. It shall be the responsibility of Purchaser, at Purchaser's expense, to satisfy himself/herself that all conditions of this contract are satisfied before closing. Said sale is contingent upon a satisfactory inspection of the property to be completed and reported to Seller prior to or on _____, 20____. Said contract shall only be renegotiable upon a major defect with an individual repair cost in excess of $500.00. After closing, all conditions of the property, as well as any aforementioned items and systems, are the responsibility of Purchaser and shall be deemed purchased AS-IS.
   (b) *Lender Required Repairs and Treatments:* Unless otherwise agreed in writing, neither party is obligated to pay for lender-required repairs, which includes treatment for wood destroying insects. If the parties do not agree to pay for the lender required repairs or treatments, this contract will terminate and the earnest money will be refunded to Purchaser. If the cost of

lender required repairs and treatments exceed 5% of the Sales Price, Purchaser may terminate this contract and the earnest money will be refunded to Purchaser.

(c) *Completion of Repairs and Treatments*: Unless otherwise agreed in writing, Seller shall complete all agreed repairs and treatments prior to the Closing Date. All required permits must be obtained, and repairs and treatments must be performed by persons who are licensed or otherwise authorized by law to provide such repairs or treatments. At Purchaser's election, any transferable warranties received by Seller with respect to the repairs and treatments will be transferred to Purchaser at Purchaser's expense. If Seller fails to complete any agreed repairs and treatments prior to the Closing Date, Purchaser may do so and receive reimbursement from Seller at closing. The Closing Date will be extended up to 15 days, if necessary, to complete repairs and treatments.

(d) *Environmental Matters:* Purchaser is advised that the presence of wetlands, toxic substances, including asbestos and wastes or other environmental hazards, or the presence of a threatened or endangered species or its habitat may affect Purchaser's intended use of the Property. If Purchaser is concerned about these matters, an addendum required by the parties should be used.

10. **SELLER WARRANTIES:** Seller warrants that Seller has not received notification from any lawful authority regarding any assessments, pending public improvements, repairs, replacements, or alterations to said premises that have not been satisfactorily made. These warranties shall survive the delivery of the above deed.

11. **EARNEST MONEY:** The Earnest Money as paid by Purchaser as set forth in Paragraph 3 hereof shall be deposited by Seller only upon the execution of this contract. The Earnest Money shall be nonrefundable to Purchaser except for the occurrences of Paragraphs 5, 6, or 14.

12. **DEFAULT:** If Purchaser fails to comply with this contract, Purchaser will be in default, and Seller may (a) enforce specific performance, seek such other relief as may be provided by law, or both, or (b) terminate this contract and receive the earnest money as liquidated damages, thereby releasing both parties from this contract. If, due to factors beyond Seller's control, Seller fails within the time allowed to make any non-casualty repairs, Purchaser may
(a) extend the time for performance up to 15 days and the Closing Date will be extended as necessary or
(b) terminate this contract as the sole remedy and receive the earnest money.

If Seller fails to comply with this contract for any other reason, Seller will be in default and Purchaser may
(a) enforce specific performance, seek such other relief as may be provided by law, or both, or
(b) terminate this contract and receive the earnest money, thereby releasing both parties from this contract.

7:1 Example Form – Real Estate Sales Contract – Private Continued

13. SURVIVAL OF CONTRACT: All terms, conditions and warranties not performed at the time of delivery of the deed shall survive such delivery.

14. COMMISSION FEES: Purchaser and Seller agree that said contract was negotiated at arms length without assistance of any real estate agents or brokers and that no such fees shall be paid by either party in connection with this contract or sale.

15. ADDITIONAL PROVISIONS: Any additional Provisions set forth on the reverse side, initialed by all parties, are hereby made a part of this contract and this contract states the entire agreement between the parties and merges in this agreement all statements, representations, and covenants heretofore made, and any agreements not incorporated herein are void and of no force and effect.

16. SUCCESSORS AND ASSIGNS: This contract shall be binding upon any heirs, successors, and assigns of Seller or Purchaser.

17. REVOCATION OF OFFER BY PURCHASER: This contract has been first executed by Purchaser and if not accepted by all parties by noon on _____, 20____, this offer shall be void.

18. DISCLOSURES: _____

_____

_____

(The Seller should note any disclosures about the property that may be required under Federal or state law. Consult an attorney if uncertainty exists as to which disclosures may be required.)

7:1 Example Form – Real Estate Sales Contract – Private Continued

This form is included for example purposes only. The form is modified from the acceptable real estate forms as released by HUD. The services of a real estate professional should be retained to ensure the correct forms are used for your transaction.

COUNTER OFFERS

Upon receiving an offer to purchase, a seller has three options.

- They may agree to the terms and conditions set forth in the offer.

  If the seller agrees to the offer for purchase, he is actually agreeing to all of the terms and conditions set forth in that offer.

  If any changes are made prior to accepting the offer, it is then considered a counter-offer.

- A counter-offer may be made by the seller and can be created by altering the terms and conditions to obtain on the original contract by crossing out the initial term, writing in a more acceptable term or condition and placing your initials beside change.

  The change must be accepted by the other party.

  Acceptance is signified by the placement of their initials beside the accepted change.

- The seller may also create a separate document that outlines the new terms of the counter-offer and present this document to the buyer for review.

- The last option available to the seller receiving an offer is to decline the offer.

  Declining the offer may result in a new offer being made on the part of the potential purchaser or it may cause the negotiations to end.

An important factor to note is that a potential buyer may withdraw their offer at any time prior to being notified that the seller has accepted the offer. This will be a rare consideration but the rights of the potential purchaser should be understood.

An example of a simple counter offer is to cross off particular points on the initial offer to purchase and write amendments to the offer, which are more desirable to the seller. To signify acceptance, both parties should initial all amendments.

The seller may choose execute a notice of counter offer, which he then signs and returns to the potential buyer with the original offer to purchase. An example of a simplified notice of counteroffer is:

NOTICE OF COUNTER OFFER

The Offer to Purchase dated _____ and signed by Buyer, _____, *(buyer name)* for purchase of real estate at_____ *(property address)* is countered. All terms and conditions to remain the same as stated on the Offer to Purchase except the following: *(Insert additional terms and conditions)*_____
_____

Seller agrees to sell and convey the above property on the terms and conditions as set forth in this Seller's Counter-Offer and acknowledges receipt of a copy of it. The warranties and representations made in this Counter-Offer survive the closing of this transaction.

7:2 Example Form – Notice of Counter Offer

This Counter-Offer must be accepted on or before _____ *(provide time and date that acceptance must be received)* and it shall not become binding upon Seller until a copy of the accepted Counter-Offer is deposited, postage prepaid, in the United States mails, addressed to Seller at _____ *(insert delivery address)* or by personal delivery thereof to Seller.

_____   _____
Signature of Seller   Signature of Seller

_____   _____
Date   Date

The above Counter-Offer is hereby (accepted/countered). If countered, all terms and conditions to remain the same as stated on the Offer to Purchase and not to include any of the terms on the above or any other Counter-Offer except the following: *(Insert additional terms and conditions)*

_____

_____

_____   _____
Signature of Buyer   Signature of Buyer

_____   _____
Date   Date

This Buyer's Counter-Offer must be accepted on or before *(provide the time and date that acceptance must be received)* and it shall not become binding upon Buyer until a copy of the accepted Counter-Offer is deposited, postage prepaid, in the United States mails, addressed to Buyer at _____ *(insert delivery address)* or by personal delivery to the Buyer.

Buyer's above Counter-Offer is hereby accepted. (If Seller is not accepting Buyer's Counter-Offer, Seller should not sign below. Seller may counter on a new Counter-Offer form.)

_____   _____
Signature of Seller   Signature of Seller

_____   _____
Date   Date

7:2 Example Form – Notice of Counter Offer - Continued
This form is included for example purposes only. The form is modified from the acceptable real estate forms as released by HUD. The services of a real estate professional should be retained to ensure the correct forms are used for your transaction.

OPTIONS

As explained earlier, an option is an agreement to keep an offer available and open for acceptance by all parties for a specified period.

One of the most popular real estate contracts is a lease with an option to buy or a lease-option.

This type of contract allows a tenant to buy the property for a specific period of time and at a specified price during the option period.

Leases, which contain this type of clause, are typically set for one year and the tenant must exercise his option to buy the property within that time or the option is void.

A lease-option simply conveys the right to purchase the property or not to purchase the property to the potential buyer for a specified period.

This option protects the potential buyer's right to time to make a decision concerning the purchase or to use the time to position themselves for the purchase.

During the option period, the contract limits the seller's ability to negotiate with another party to transfer the property. In other words, the property is "tied up" for the option period.

An option may require option consideration or a stipend payment to secure the option be made at the time of signing.

An option may also require that a certain premium be paid at regular intervals throughout the option period to maintain the option rights.

These payments may be refundable or non-refundable and are open for negotiation between the seller and the potential buyer.

A lease option is simply a combination between a lease agreement and an option agreement.

A lease option is typically formatted to include all the normal provisions of a residential real estate lease.

It also incorporates the normal provisions of a purchase agreement with a statement that the tenant is given the right of exercising his option to purchase the property at the given terms providing the tenant notifies the landlord of the decision to exercise his option in writing during the agreed upon option period.

All terms of the lease and the purchase contract must be negotiated in writing before the signing of the contract and both the tenant/buyer and landlord/seller must sign the agreement.

A section outlining the acceptable terms of financing will be included in the contract.

The seller may agree to implement an installment contract, which is also termed land contract, article of agreement, contract for deed or variations of these names or the seller may require outside financing be obtained.

In either event, the seller will sometimes agree to "give-back" a certain portion of the rental payments toward the sales price.

This is completed in the form of a down payment acknowledgement. If the tenant does not exercise his right to purchase during the option period, this additional sum paid toward a potential down payment is typically given to the seller in consideration of the offer of the option.

The handling of any funds paid in surplus of regulated monthly rental should be clearly negotiated on the fully executed and signed lease-option contract.

A lease-option agreement can be set for any term that is acceptable for both the landlord/seller and the tenant/buyer.

These types of contracts typically do not extend beyond a year for residential property.

Each negotiation will contain variations, which are negotiable points, and the term of the option is one such negotiating point.

A seller/landlord may also negotiate a one time or multi-payment option fee.

It is important that any fees make sense from the perspective of the tenant/buyer.

The seller should consult an accountant to determine what, if any, tax consequences may result from a contract of this type.

This type of offer is not used only for residential rental property but is also particularly attractive to sellers in a soft real estate market or a market where home sales are slow.

In a slow market, a seller who desires the sale of a property may simply lower the purchase price or they may offer seller-financing terms.

Seller financing terms are attractive to buyers and aid in selling a property more quickly.

At times, the seller will want to wait out the market conditions to obtain better terms and sales price when the market solidifies.

In the event the seller must vacate or sell the property before the market turns, the lease with the option to buy premise is often a very attractive option.

This option allows a seller facing these circumstances to lease the property for a term to a tenant who is also a perspective buyer and will therefore be more serious in the payment for and upkeep of the property.

This lease agreement allows the seller to

- turn the upkeep and occupancy of the property over to another

- receive the stipend payment to offset the costs of the property

- secure a potential buyer at the terms the seller desires

If the option is exercised by the tenant, the seller has accomplished his goal of obtaining a higher purchase price on the property than he may have realized in a soft market and in the event the tenant does not exercise the option the seller is then able to list the property for sale in a hopefully improved market.

The act of applying a portion of the rental payment toward the purchase price is used as an inducement to encourage the tenant to exercise the option and is not always included as part of the option.

This is a negotiable point, which will vary with each contract.

When negotiating a rental payment give back with an eye toward conventional finance it is important to understand the parameters of the financing the potential buyers may attempt to secure in the future.

Many underwriting departments are willing to accept lease-option terms as sourced down payment funds but may limit the dollar amount of rental payment that can be claimed as part of the down payment funds held toward the purchase.

This limitation typically states that the amount of the monthly rental, which can be credited toward down payment funds, is limited to the difference between fair market rent for a similar property in the area and the actual payment made by the tenant/buyer.

Example: If the fair market rent for a property is judged to be $300 monthly and the tenant/buyer pays only $300 monthly as their lease option payment many underwriters will not accept any portion of the payment as credit toward the purchase price.

If the fair market rent for a property is judged to be $300 monthly and the tenant pays $400 monthly many underwriters will accept the $100 in rent paid monthly that is judged to be in excess of the typical fair market rent for a similar property in that area to be an amount paid toward down payment.

OPTION AGREEMENT FOR PURCHASE OF REAL PROPERTY

THIS OPTION AGREEMENT ("Agreement") made and entered into this _____ day of _____, 20_____, by and between _____, whose principal address is _____, hereinafter referred to as "Seller" and _____, whose principal address is _____, hereinafter referred to as "Purchaser":

W I T N E S S E T H:

WHEREAS, Seller is the fee simple owner of certain real property being, lying and situated in the County of _____, State of _____, such real property having the street address of _____ ("Premises") and such property being more particularly described as follows: _____and,

WHEREAS, Purchaser desires to procure an option to purchase the Premises upon the terms and provisions as hereinafter set forth;

NOW, THEREFORE, for good and valuable consideration the receipt and sufficiency of which is hereby acknowledged by the parties hereto and for the mutual covenants contained herein, Seller and Purchaser hereby agree as follows:

1. DEFINITIONS For the purposes of this Agreement, the following terms shall have the following meanings:
    (a) "Execution Date" shall mean the day upon which the last party to this Agreement shall duly execute this Agreement
    (b) "Option Fee" shall mean the total sum of a down payment of _____ percent (___%) of the total purchase price of the Premises plus all closing costs, payable as set forth below;
    (c) "Option Term" shall mean that period of time commencing on the Execution Date and ending on or before _____, 20____
    (d) "Option Exercise Date" shall mean that date, within the Option Term, upon which the Purchaser shall send its written notice to Seller exercising its Option to Purchase
    (e) "Closing Date" shall mean the last day of the closing term or such other date during the closing term selected by Purchaser.

2. GRANT OF OPTION. For and in consideration of the Option Fee payable to Seller as set forth herein, Seller does hereby grant to Purchaser the exclusive right and Option ("Option") to purchase the premises upon the terms and conditions as set forth herein.

3. PAYMENT OF OPTION FEE Purchaser agrees to pay the Seller a down payment of _____ percent (____%) of the total purchase price of the Premises plus all closing costs upon the Execution Date.

7:3 Example Form – Option to Purchase

4. EXERCISE OF OPTION Purchaser may exercise its exclusive right to purchase the Premises pursuant to the Option, at any time during the Option Term, by giving written notice thereof to Seller. As provided for above, the date of sending of said notice shall be the Option Exercise Date. In the event the Purchaser does not exercise its exclusive right to purchase the Premises granted by the Option during the Option Term, Seller shall be entitled to retain the Option Fee, and this agreement shall become absolutely null and void and neither party hereto shall have any other liability, obligation, or duty herein under or pursuant to this Agreement.

5. CONTRACT FOR PURCHASE & SALE OF REAL PROPERTY In the event that the Purchaser exercises its exclusive Option as provided for in the preceding paragraph, Seller agrees to sell and Purchaser agrees to buy the Premises and both parties agree to execute a contract for such purchase and sale of the Premises in accordance with the following terms and conditions:

    (a) Purchase Price. The purchase price for the Premises shall be the sum of _____ ($_____); however, Purchaser shall receive a credit toward such purchase price in the amount of the Option Fee thus, Purchaser shall pay to Seller at closing the sum of _____ ($_____);

    (b) Closing Date The closing date shall be on _____, 20____ or at any other date during the Option Term as may be selected by Purchaser

    (c) Closing Costs Purchaser's and Seller's costs of closing the Contract shall be borne by Purchase and shall be prepaid as a portion of the Option Fee;

    (d) Default by Purchaser; Remedies of Seller. In the event Purchaser, after exercise of the Option, fails to proceed with the closing of the purchase of the Premises pursuant to the terms and provisions as contained herein and/or under the Contract, Seller shall be entitled to retain the Option Fee as liquidated damages and shall have no further recourse against Purchaser;

    (e) Default by Seller; Remedies of Purchaser. In the event Seller fails to close the sale of the Premises pursuant to the terms and provisions of this Agreement and/or under the Contract, Purchaser shall be entitled to either sue for specific performance of the real estate purchase and sale contract or terminate such Contract and sue for money damages.

6. MISCELLANEOUS

    (a) Execution by Both Parties This Agreement shall not become effective and binding until fully executed by both Purchaser and Seller.

    (b) Notice All notices, demands, and/or consents provided for in this Agreement shall be in writing and shall be delivered to the parties hereto by hand or by United States Mail with postage pre-paid. Such notices shall be deemed to have been served on the date mailed, postage pre-paid. All such notices and communications shall be addressed to the Seller at _____ and to Purchaser at _____ or at such other address as either may specify to the other in writing.

    (c) Fee Governing Law This Agreement shall be governed by and construed in accordance with the laws of the State of _____.

    (d) Successors and Assigns This Agreement shall apply to, inure to the benefit of, and be binding upon and enforceable against the parties hereto and their respective heirs, successors, and or assigns, to the extent as if specified at length throughout this Agreement.

    (e) Time is of the essence of this Agreement.

    (f) Headings The headings inserted at the beginning of each paragraph and/or subparagraph are for convenience of reference only and shall not limit or otherwise affect or be used in the construction of any terms or provisions hereof.

    (g) Cost of this Agreement Any cost and/or fees incurred by the Purchaser or Seller in executing this Agreement shall be borne by the respective party incurring such cost and/or fee.

7:3 Example Form – Option to Purchase Continued

(h) Entire Agreement This Agreement contains all of the terms, promises, covenants, conditions and representations made or entered into by or between Seller and Purchaser and supersedes all prior discussions and agreements whether written or oral between Seller and Purchaser with respect to the Option and all other matters contained herein and constitutes the sole and entire agreement between Seller and Purchaser with respect thereto. This Agreement may not be modified or amended unless such amendment is set forth in writing and executed by both Seller and Purchaser with the formalities hereof.

IN WITNESS WHEREOF, the parties hereto have caused this Agreement to be executed under proper authority:
As to Purchaser this _____ day of _____, 20_____
Witnesses: "Purchaser"

_____   _____

As to Seller this _____ day of _____, 20_____
Witnesses: "Seller"

_____   _____

7:3 Example Form – Option to Purchase Continued

This form is included for example purposes only. The form is modified from the acceptable real estate forms as released by HUD. The services of a real estate professional should be retained to ensure the correct forms are used for your transaction.

TENANT'S NOTICE TO EXERCISE PURCHASE OPTION

Date: _____

To: _____

Dear _____:

Notice is hereby provided that the undersigned as Lessee under a certain Lease dated _____, 20_____, does hereby exercise its purchase option under said lease to purchase the property described as _____
_____ for the option price of $_____.

As contained within the lease agreement I enclose $_____ as a deposit toward said purchase option.

_____
Lessee Signature

7:4 Example Form – Tenant's Notice to Exercise Option
This form is included for example purposes only. The form is modified from the acceptable real estate forms as released by HUD. The services of a real estate professional should be retained to ensure the correct forms are used for your transaction.

EXTENDING AN OPTION

At times, the negotiated option period may expire before a finalized sale can be executed. At that time, the parties may renegotiate the terms of the option and enact an entire new option agreement or they may simply enact an agreement to extend the option term. This is a point that should be negotiated at the time the original lease option is written.

Negotiating possible extension terms and conditions at the first agreement period limit potential problems later in the transaction. The following agreement extending the period of option sets forth the simple terms required for extending the options. This is a sample agreement and you should retain the services of a real estate professional to ensure that the contract you use is customized to your particular transaction.

AGREEMENT EXTENDING PERIOD OF OPTION

In consideration of the additional sum of _____ Dollars ($_____) paid to
_____, referred to as seller, by _____, referred to as purchaser, the period of that certain option from seller to purchaser dated,
_____ is hereby extended to _____ (date).

This extension shall apply to all provisions, and conditions of the option shall acclimate to purchaser, and purchaser's heirs, nominees. In witness whereof, the parties have brought about this instrument twofold at_____ (place of implementation) on _____ (date).

_____   _____   _____
Signature   Title   Date

_____   _____   _____
Signature   Title   Date

7:5 Example Form – Agreement Extending Period of Option

This form is included for example purposes only. The form is modified from the acceptable real estate forms as released by HUD. The services of a real estate professional should be retained to ensure the correct forms are used for your transaction.

Agreement to Lease With Option to Purchase

Parties:

Buyer _____ of _____

and

Seller_____ of_____

In consideration of the payments, covenants, agreements and conditions herein contained the above parties hereby agree to lease with an option the following property:

Subject: Property Address:_____

Legal Description: _____

_____

Personal Property _____

Personal property to be transferred at closing by bill of sale free of any encumbrances.

Existing Loans- At time of closing buyer may elect to take title subject to the existing loans to_____

In the amount of $_____ bearing interest rate of _____% payable _____ (P&I)

Or the loan will be paid off by the seller.

Loan Number_____ Date last payment made_____

Other Liens, back taxes, etc._____

Term of lease and option _____months beginning _____

Monthly Payment $_____due on the _____day of each month beginning_____ 20_____

Monthly credit toward purchase price when rent paid on time $_____

Purchase Price $_____, additional option consideration _____to apply towards purchase price.

1. TERMS: Seller agrees that upon the exercise of the option they will assist in financing by taking as part of the purchase price a note in the amount of $_____ with payments of $_____ beginning _____.

2. MAINTENANCE: The buyers shall pay for all repairs costing less than $ 100.00 each month. Repairs costing $100 or more will be paid by the owner. Should the owner fail to make repairs to maintain the house in its current condition, the buyer may have said repairs made and receive a credit equal to 200% of the cost of the repair toward the purchase price and a full credit toward the next payment due.

3. SELLER'S AGREEMENT NOT TO FURTHER ENCUMBER: Sellers agree not to refinance the property, nor to modify any existing loans, nor to transfer any interest in the property during the term of this agreement.

4. PAYMENTS ON EXISTING LOANS, TAXES AND INSURANCE: Seller shall be responsible for paying the taxes, loan payments and for keeping the property insured for its full replacement value during the term of this agreement. In the event seller fails to make payments when due of taxes, insurance, or loan payments, buyer may elect to make said pays due payments and receive 200% of their amount credited toward the purchase price and full credit toward the next payment due the seller.

5. PRORATIONS: Taxes, insurance, and loan interest shall be prorated as of the date of closing of the purchase.

7:6 Example Form – Lease with Option to Purchase

6. BUYER & SELLER: agree to fully execute and place in escrow with _____ instruments needed to convey title. The seller shall deposit and executed warranty deed, and copies of existing mortgages, notes, title insurance policies, and surveys. Buyer shall deposit an executed quitclaim deed that will be delivered to the seller in the event of default by the buyer under this contract. All agree to sign an escrow agreement that will empower the escrow agent to close the transaction if all terms of the contract are met, and that will hold the agent harmless.

7. TRANSFER OF TITLE: In the event buyer chooses to exercise their option to purchase, they will notify the seller during the term of this agreement. Within 15 days of receipt of such notice, sellers agree to convey good and marketable title, free from all encumbrances except those that a buyer wishes to take title subject to. Sellers further agree to furnish an owner's title binder within 5 days after receiving notice, showing no exceptions other than as listed above, and furnish a policy of title insurance at closing.

8. DAMAGES: In the event seller fails to perform, buyer will be entitled to recover all monies paid on this agreement, and may pursue all other legal remedies available. Seller will be responsible for all costs including a reasonable attorney's fee. In the event buyer fails to exercise the option, all option consideration, and rents paid will be forfeited as full-liquidated damages.

9. RECORDING: All parties agree that this agreement or a memorandum including any parts of their agreement acceptable to the buyer may be recorded.

10. SUCCESSORS AND ASSIGNS & SUBLETTING: The terms and conditions of this contract shall bind all successors, heirs, administrators, executors, assigns, and those subletting.

11. ACCESS AND ADVERTISING: Sellers agree that the buyer may advertise the property and shall immediately have access during reasonable hours to show the property to others.

12. TIME IS OF THE ESSENCE IN ALL MATTERS OF THE AGREEMENT

13. OTHER TERMS:

    _____
    _____
    _____
    _____
    _____

The undersigned agree to buy and sell on the above terms, have-read, fully understand and verify the above information as being correct. All parties acknowledge that this is a legally binding contract and are advised to seek the counsel of an attorney.

7:6 Example Form – Lease with Option to Purchase Continued

This form is included for example purposes only. The form is modified from the acceptable real estate forms as released by HUD. The services of a real estate professional should be retained to ensure the correct forms are used for your transaction.

INSTALLMENT CONTRACT

An installment contract, contract for deed, land contract, article of agreement, or conditional sales contract combines the features of a sales agreement, a deed, and a mortgage into one basic contract.

Most of the points of a standard sales agreement are incorporated into this contract. Information regarding the deed and provisions of the mortgage are also included.

Using a contract such as this aid in the simplification of a creative finance scenario as more of the documentation and negotiation points are included on the initial agreement and fewer additional contracts will be required.

An important factor with an installment contract is whether the seller is delivering the actual deed to the buyer at closing.

A contract of this type allows a promise on the part of the seller to deliver the deed to the buyer at some future time contingent upon the performance of the terms of the contract by the buyer.

This must be clearly stated in the agreement between the buyer and seller so all parties has adequate expectations and a full understanding of the obligations and responsibilities concerning the deed.

Even though the deed is being escrowed, the buyer is given all the rights of ownership typical of a real estate sale such as the right to occupy the property and to fulfill all obligations of the property but is not obtaining the actual deed until the end of the transaction term.

Contracts of this type are often used in situations where the buyer is unable to pay the entire purchase price, either in cash, goods, and services, using a mortgage or by other means, at the time of sale.

In lieu of a cash payoff, the seller accepts a down payment and monthly installment payments toward the purchase price.

The terms of sale will be negotiated on a case-by-case basis and the seller may deliver the deed at closing much like in any other transaction and at the same moment take a promissory note and mortgage from the buyer.

The parties also may enter into an installment contract requiring the buyer to make all payments agreed upon before the deed is delivered.

One of the primary negotiable points of this type of contract is the down payment.

This is the up-front premium paid from the buyer to the seller as a means of providing security to the seller that the buyer intends to complete the transaction.

Conventional lenders follow the premise of assuming the higher the amount of the down payment (vested interest) on the part of the buyer, the lower the likelihood of default.

In non-conventional and creative financing scenarios, it is important to remember that buyers frequently seek out these finance options when they are unable to meet the requirements set by the conventional mortgage market with regards to down payment.

The down payment is often a strong point in the negotiation process and to obtain a successful transaction the seller may need to obtain their security against default through other measures such as a higher interest rate return.

Periodic payments are also typically negotiated.

A periodic payment (often monthly) will typically include the interest payment and an amount toward principal though these can be principal only payments, fully amortized payments, interest only payments or any other type of payment agreed to by the parties.

At times, a balloon payment is agreed upon between the buyer and the seller.

A balloon payment may follow a period of periodic payments or stand-alone.

A balloon payment is simply a one-time payment of the balance due at the end of the contract term.

Balloon payments are frequently negotiated as a means of limiting the term the seller will carry the mortgage.

They are often used when a specified number of months principal payment are needed to meet conventional lending guidelines or a period of time is needed by the buyer to qualify of conventional financing. During this waiting period, the seller may obtain principal and interest payments.

When set balloon term has elapsed, the negotiated balloon ensures the seller of a cash-out.

Often balloon payments are written into the negotiation even when the amortization of the mortgage is spread over a longer term.

Example: a property selling at $50,000 with a balloon payment of all balances due after 5 years may be negotiated if the seller feels they are unable to hold the mortgage longer than the five-year period.

It would be a hardship for many buyers to make payments on a mortgage amortized over only five years so the seller may agree to amortize the payments over 30 years. This longer amortization will lower the monthly amount required from the buyer.

The contract would also call for a balloon of the balance after 5 years, therefore ensuring the sellers cash out within the specified period.

In some contracts, periodic balloon payments are negotiated.

These payments occur at specified points throughout the contract term.

These payments can be applied to principal, principal and interest, or in some other manner as negotiated under the agreement between the buyer and seller.

Periodic balloon payments are frequently used in the negotiations if the buyers are unable to provide a sufficient down payment at the beginning of the contract.

The variety and combinations of negotiated points are tremendous and are limited only to the abilities of the involved parties to remain creative and negotiate to reach a settlement that provides for the needs of both parties.

The installment or land contract was typically used in the past for the transfer of land transactions. Over time, the use of this style of contract moved into the private finance of other types of real estate. As the transaction style gained popularity, many states began implementing protective measures required for inclusion in the installment contracts.

Historically, installment contracts were weighted in the favor of the seller.

Some states have now implemented regulations which require that installment contracts be recorded at the courthouse and that they must be foreclosed using conventional means rather than utilizing clauses and addendum's written into the contract that relinquish the buyers rights immediately in the event of non-performance. The laws governing the exact methods used in installment contracts vary by state and before considering this type of contract, they should be properly researched. It is always suggested that the services of a reliable real estate attorney or other real estate professional be used in the drafting and enforcing of an installment contract.

Regardless of the specifics, many installment contracts share the same qualities.

- the name of the buyer

- the name of seller

- the sales price

- terms of payment

- a full legal description of the property

are the first components to be included.

Additionally, the sales price and the terms of use and maintenance of the property are typically listed on the contract.

The contract can be a one-step process, which includes the purchase offer, acceptance of the offer plus the finance agreement and delivery protocols for the payments and the deed.

The purchase agreement may negotiate the sale and terms similar to any other real estate purchase agreement with the specifics of action after the sale being included on a separate document, which then becomes the installment contract.

Land Contract

This Agreement is made and entered into by and between _____ (seller), whose address is,_____
hereinafter called the Vendor and _____ (buyer) whose address is _____
hereinafter called the Vendee.

Witnesseth: The Vendor, for himself, his heirs and assigns, does hereby agree to sell to the Vendee, their heirs and assigns, the following real estate commonly known as:_____
_____ and further described; as _____
_____together with all appurtenances, rights, privileges, easements, and all buildings and fixtures in their present condition located upon said property.

1.   CONTRACT PRICE METHOD OF PAYMENT, INTEREST RATE:

In consideration whereof, the Vendee agrees to purchase the above-described property for the sum of
_____ Dollars
($_____), payable as follows:

The sum of $_____ as initial consideration at the time of execution of the within Land Contract, the receipt of which is hereby acknowledged, leaving a principal balance owed by Vendee of $_____ together with interest on the unpaid balance payable in consecutive monthly installments of $_____ beginning on the _____ day of _____20____, and on the _____ day of each and every month thereafter until said balance and interest is paid in full, or until the _____ day of _____ 20_____
at which time the entire remaining balance plus accrued interest shall become due and payable.

The interest on the unpaid balance due hereon shall be (_____ %) percent annum computed monthly, in accordance with a month amortization schedule during the life of this agreement.

Payments shall be credited first to the interest. The remainder to the principal or other sums due Vendor. The total amount of this obligation, both principal and interest, unpaid after making any such application of payments as herein receipted shall be the interest bearing principal amount of this obligation for the next succeeding interest computation period. If any payment is not received within _____ (_____) days of payment date, there shall be a late charge of (_____ %) percent assessed.

7:7 Example Form – Installment Land Contract

The Vendees may pay the entire purchase price on this contract without prepayment penalty. The monthly installments shall be payable as directed by the Vendor herein.

2. ENCUMBRANCES:
Said real estate is presently subject to a mortgage with_____ and the Vendor shall not place any additional mortgage on the premises without the prior written permission of the Vendees.

Vendee may elect at any time to pay any sums due hereunder directly to the mortgagee, and any amounts remaining to the Vendor.

Vendor understands that this transaction may permit the mortgagee to exercise their right to accelerate the loan and to call the remaining balance due. In any such event, the Vendor agrees to hold Vendee harmless and in no way liable for any damage to Vendor because of such action. Vendor initials _____.

3. EVIDENCE OF TITLE:
The Vendor shall be required to provide an abstract or guarantee of title, statement of title, title insurance, or such other evidence of title to Vendee's satisfaction.

4. RECORDING OF CONTRACT:

The Vendor shall permit a copy of this contract to be recorded in the _____County Recorder's Office at Vendee's discretion at any time subsequent to the execution of this Contract by the parties hereto.

5. REAL ESTATE TAXES:
Real estate taxes to the County Treasurer shall remain In the Vendor's name throughout the term of this agreement. Payment of said taxes shall be the responsibility of the Vendee upon the execution of this agreement, and [____] shall [____] shall not be escrowed and added to the payment required by Vendee herein.

6. INSURANCE AND MAINTENANCE:
The Vendor shall insure the property with a non owner-occupant (landlord) policy against fire and extended coverage to the benefit of both parties as their Interests may appear herein. Said policy shall be for an amount no less than _____, payment of which shall be the responsibility of the Vendee, and which shall be escrowed and added to the payment due herein.

Vendees shall keep the building in a good state of repair at the Vendees expense. At such time as the Vendor inspects the premises and finds that repairs are necessary, Vendor shall request that these repairs be made within sixty (60) days at the Vendees expense.

The Vendees have inspected the premises constituting the subject matter of this Land Contract, and no representations have been made to the Vendee by the Vendor in regard to the condition of said premises: and it is agreed that the said premises are being sold to the Vendee as the same now exists and that the Vendor shall have no obligation to do or furnish anything toward the improvement of said premises.

Vendor shall furnish a clear termite report at Vendor's expense prior to executing this contract. If the property has live infestation of wood destroying insec1s, Vendor will pay costs of treatment and repair damages caused by same. If Vendor elects not to do so. Vendee may elect to waive Vendors responsibility and proceed. Vendee may elect not to proceed with this contract. Notice of each election shall be given in writing within five (5) days of. respectively. receipt of Vendor of the notice of infestation and receipt by Vendee of Vendors notice as to intention to remedy.

7:7 Example Form – Installment Land Contract Continued

7. POSSESSION
The Vendee shall be given possession of the above described premises at Contract execution and shall thereafter have and hold the same subject to default provisions hereinafter set forth.

8. Delivery of DEED:
Upon full payment of this contract, Vendor shall issue a General Warranty deed to the Vendees free of all encumbrances except as otherwise set forth. In addition, Vendees reserves the right to convert this contract into a note and mortgage which shall bear the same terms as the contract for the remaining balance, and receive a warranty Deed to Vendees or assigns from Vendor, anytime the following conditions have been met by then Vendees,

1. At least 20% of the purchase price has been paid to the Vendor.
2. Vendee is willing to pay all the costs of title transfer and document preparations.

9. DEFAULT BY VENDEES
If an installment payment to be made by the Vendee under the terms of this Land Contract is not paid by the Vendee when due or within thirty (30) days thereafter, the entire unpaid balance shall become due and collectable at the election of the Vendor and the Vendor shall be entitled to all the remedies provided for by the laws of this state and/or to do any other remedies and/or seek relief now or hereafter provided for by law to such Vendor; and in the event of the breach of this contract in any other respect by the Vendee, Vendor shall be entitled to all relief now or hereinafter provided for by the laws of this state.

Failure of Vendee to maintain current the status of all real estate taxes and insurance premiums as required herein shall permit Vendor the option to pay any such premiums, taxes, interest, or penalty (ies), and to add the amount paid to the principal amount owing under this contract, or to exercise any remedies available to the Vendor as per the preceding paragraph.

Waiver by the Vendor of a default or a number of defaults in the performance hereof by the Vendee shall not be construed as a waiver of any future default no matter how similar.

10. GENERAL PROVISIONS:

There are no known pending orders issued by any governmental authority with respect to this property other than those spelled out in this Land Contract prior to closing date for the execution of the contract.

11. SPECIAL PROVISIONS:
_____
_____
_____

12. ENTIRE AGREEMENT:
It is agreed that this instrument and any addendum mutually entered into and, by reference to this agreement, made a part hereof constitutes the entire agreement of the parties, and which shall be binding upon each of the parties, their administrators. executors, heirs, and assigns. It is further agreed that neither party is relying upon any representation not contained herein.

7:7 Example Form – Installment Land Contract

DOWNPAYMENT/LUMP SUM PAYMENTS

When the terms and conditions of the sale of real estate have been agreed upon the first payment to the seller will typically take the form of a down payment.

The amount of the down payment will be a factor in the negotiations.

Down payments are utilized to provide the seller with an immediate income from the sale as well as to offer security that the buyer will not default on future payments.

In standard lending, the probability of default is measured, in part, by the amount of their own cash buyers have invested in the property.

The general theory is that the more money a borrower has at risk the less likely they are to default.

The down payment amount is a prime negotiating point as some buyers may not have a large amount of ready cash for the purchase of a home or they may desire to keep their cash in hand for renovations to the new property or even the purchase of furniture and other items needed upon move-in at the new property.

At times, the seller may be willing to be flexible on the terms of the down payment monies required in return for other negotiating points that are in the sellers favor such as interest rate.

Upon receipt of the down payment, it is advisable to create an additional document or addendum.

This document acknowledges the receipt of the down payment monies and states how the down payment funds are to be applied.

In most cases, any down payment funds received are applied to the principal amount of the purchase price of the property.

If the contract between the buyer and seller calls for periodic payments in addition to the initial down payment and the monthly mortgage payments, these additional payments should also be allocated in the negotiated agreement.

The buyer and seller should state clearly, when the payments are due and exactly how they will be applied to the loan.

Example: will the payments be applied directly to principal and if so, will the loan be re-amortized to reflect the payment of the additional lump sum?

Regardless of the terms outlined for the handling of the lump sum payments, it is advisable to create an additional document or addendum reflecting the payment.

This document should acknowledge the receipt of the lump sum monies and state how the funds are to be applied to the contract.

The acknowledgement of receipt can take many forms. The following sample may be customized to suit the situation and is a general form of an acknowledgement receipt. As always, it is best to consult a real estate professional or reliable attorney when composing any legal document.

ACKNOWLEDGMENT DOWN PAYMENT ON PURCHASE

The following shall be considered a legally binding amendment to the agreement made between
_____ and _____ ,
dated _____ , for the sale of _____ :
Of the purchase price, _____ Dollars is paid this _____ day of _____ (month),
_____ (year), as a down payment, which shall be credited to the purchase price after completion of the transaction. Seller acknowledges receipt of this down payment.

_____   _____
Signature   Date

_____   _____
Signature   Date

_____   _____
Witness   Date

_____

7:8 Example Form – Acknowledgement Down Payment on Purchase
This form is included for example purposes only. The form is modified from the acceptable real estate forms as released by HUD. The services of a real estate professional should be retained to ensure the correct forms are used for your transaction.

MORTGAGE ASSUMPTION

At times, the seller may have secured a mortgage on a property that allows for the assumption of the mortgage by another party.

This means the buyer will sign documents with the mortgage holder.

In this scenario, the mortgage holder is the original lender of the funds to the seller.

By signing these documents, the buyer effectively takes the seller's place in the mortgage and note agreements and removes the seller's obligations to pay the mortgage holder.

Not all mortgages are assumable. The ability to perform this type of transfer depends on the terms the original lender set.

The seller should carefully read their mortgage documents to determine if this is a potential option. In the event the mortgage may be assumed by a new buyer, the lender or mortgage holder will usually require the buyer to meet certain eligibility criteria.

Even when the existing mortgage is assumed, the seller may require additional funds from the buyer towards the purchase of the property.

These additional funds are typically equal to the amount of equity (value – mortgage = equity) the seller holds in the property.

Because a conventional lender is involved, there may be certain minimum requirements set forth concerning the amount of cash a new borrower must invest up front or the maximum amount of a second mortgage the seller may hold against the property. These issues should be discussed with a loan officer from the original lending institution and then negotiated, according to the original lender restrictions, between the buyer and the seller.

An example of a simplified clause negotiating the assumption plus a cash balance owed in one lump sum is detailed on the following page. A variation of this clause may be created if the buyer and seller agree that the seller will receive their cash portion of the sales price in monthly payments or another negotiated term and held by a 2nd mortgage and note.   This example form is a broad form and as always, the services of a real estate attorney or other competent professional should be retained when creating any contract.

LOAN ASSUMPTION ADDENDUM

TO CONTRACT CONCERNING THE PROPERTY AT: (*Address of Property*) _____
_____

A. **CREDIT DOCUMENTATION:** Within _____ days after the effective date of this contract,

Purchaser shall deliver to Seller the following: (*check all applicable items:*)
_____ Credit report
_____ Verification of employment, including salary
_____ Verification of funds on deposit in financial institutions
_____ Current financial statement to establish Purchaser's creditworthiness
_____ Other: _____
Purchaser hereby authorizes any credit-reporting agency to furnish to Seller at Purchaser's sole expense copies of Purchaser's credit reports. _____ Signature

B. **CREDIT APPROVAL:** If Purchaser's documentation is not delivered within the specified time, Seller may terminate this contract by notice to Purchaser within 7 days after expiration of the time for delivery, and the earnest money will be paid to Seller.

7:8 Example Form - Loan Assumption Addendum

If the documentation is timely delivered, and Seller determines in Seller's sole discretion that Purchaser's credit is unacceptable, Seller may terminate this contract by notice to Purchaser within 7 days after expiration of the time for delivery and the earnest money will be refunded to Purchaser.

If Seller does not terminate this contract, Seller will be deemed to have accepted Purchaser's credit.

C. ASSUMPTION:

_____ (1) The unpaid principal balance of a first lien promissory note payable to which unpaid balance at closing will be $_____. The total current monthly payment including principal, interest and any reserve deposits is $_____. Purchaser's initial payment will be the first payment due after closing.

_____ (2) The unpaid principal balance of a second lien promissory note payable to which unpaid balance at closing will be $_____. The total current monthly payment including principal, interest and any reserve deposits is $_____. Purchaser's initial payment will be the first payment due after closing.   Purchaser's assumption of an existing note includes all obligations imposed by the deed of trust securing the note. If the unpaid principal balance(s) of any assumed loan(s) as of the Closing Date varies from the loan balance(s) stated above, the (*check only one:*)

_____ Cash payable at closing

_____ Sales Price will be adjusted by the amount of any variance; provided, if the total principal balance of all assumed loans varies in an amount greater than $350.00 at closing, either party may terminate this contract and the earnest money will be refunded to Purchaser unless the other party elects to eliminate the excess in the variance by an appropriate adjustment at closing. Purchaser may terminate this contract and the earnest money will be refunded to Purchaser if the note holder requires

(a)   payment of an assumption fee in excess of $_____ in (1) above or $_____ in (2) above and Seller declines to pay such excess,

(b)   an increase in the interest rate to more than _____% in (1) above, or _____% in (2) above,

(c)   any other modification of the loan documents, or

(d)   consent to the assumption of the loan and fails to consent. An appropriate instrument authorized within the state, typically either (1) a mortgage or (2) vendor's and deed of trust liens, to secure the assumption will be required, and it will automatically be released on execution and delivery of a release by note holder. If Seller is released from liability on any assumed note, the instrument securing the assumption will not be required. If note holder maintains an escrow account, the escrow account must be transferred to Purchaser without any deficiency. Purchaser shall reimburse Seller for the amount in the transferred accounts.

NOTICE TO PURCHASER: The monthly payments, interest rates or other terms of some loans may be adjusted by the note holder at or after closing. If you are concerned about the possibility of future adjustments, do not sign the contract without examining the notes and the instrument securing the note.

NOTICE TO SELLER: Your liability to pay the note assumed by Purchaser will continue unless you obtain a release of liability from the note holder. If you are concerned about future liability, you should use the Release of Liability Addendum.

7:8 Example Form - Loan Assumption Addendum Continued

This form is included for example purposes only. The form is modified from the acceptable real estate forms as released by HUD. The services of a real estate professional should be retained to ensure the correct forms are used for your transaction.

MORTGAGE ASSUMPTION AGREEMENT

THIS MORTGAGE ASSUMPTION AGREEMENT (hereinafter referred to as the "Agreement") made and entered into as of this __ day of _____, 20__, by and between _____, of _____, (hereinafter referred to as the "Lender") and _____, of _____ (hereinafter referred to as "Borrower").

WITNESSETH:

WHEREAS, Lender is the holder and owner of the following documents (hereinafter sometimes collectively referred to as the "Loan Documents"):

1. Mortgage Note dated _____, in the original principal face amount of _____ DOLLARS ($_____) executed and delivered by _____ (hereinafter referred to as the "Original Borrower") in favor of Lender (hereinafter referred to as the "Note"); and,

2. Mortgage given by Original Borrower as "Mortgagor" to Lender as "Mortgagee" dated _____, which Mortgage is recorded on the Public Records of _____ County, _____ at O.R. Book __, Page __ (hereinafter referred to as the "Mortgage"), and which Mortgage encumbers the real property as described therein; and,

WHEREAS, the Original Borrower is desirous of conveying the property encumbered by the Mortgage, (hereinafter referred to as the "Property") to Borrower; and,

WHEREAS, the Borrower desires to receive said Property and formally assume the Mortgage and perform all of the covenants and conditions contained in the Mortgage Note, the Mortgage and all other Loan Documents as partial consideration for its purchase of the Property and as consideration for the Lender's willingness to consent to the sale of the Property which is encumbered by the Loan Documents; and,

WHEREAS, the Mortgage expressly prohibits the conveyance of the Property without the express written consent of the Lender; and,

WHEREAS, the Lender is unwilling to give its consent to the transfer of the Property to the Borrower unless the Borrower shall assume all of the obligations heretofore imposed by the Loan Documents upon the Original Borrower

NOW, THEREFORE, for and in consideration of the sum of _____DOLLARS ($_____) and in consideration of the Premises and of the mutual covenants contained herein, and for other good and valuable considerations, the receipt and sufficiency of which are hereby acknowledged by the parties, the parties hereto agree as follows:

1. Assumption Borrower expressly assumes the Loan Documents and agrees to perform all covenants, conditions, duties, and obligations contained therein and agree to pay the Note and the obligations evidenced thereby in a prompt and timely manner in accordance with the terms thereof.
2. Consent to Conveyance. Lender hereby consents to the transfer of the Property to the Borrower, but the Lender expressly reserves the right to withhold its consent to any future sale or transfer of the Property, as provided for in the Mortgage.
3. Warranties and Representations Borrower affirms, warrants, represents, and covenants that Borrower has neither defenses nor rights of set-off against Lender or against the payment, collection, or enforcement of

7:9 Example Form - Mortgage Assumption Agreement

the indebtedness evidenced by the Note and secured by the Mortgage and owed to Lender. Borrower further warrants and represents as follows:

a. Borrower has done no acts nor omitted to do any act which might prevent Lender from, or limit Lender in, acting upon or under any of the provisions herein, in the Mortgage, in the Note or any other Loan Documents

b. Borrower is not prohibited under any other agreement with any other person or any judgment or decree, from the execution and delivery of this Agreement, the performance of each and every covenant hereunder or under the Mortgage, Note or any other Loan Documents

c. No action has been brought or threatened which would in any way interfere with the right of Borrower to execute this Agreement and perform all of Borrower's obligations contained herein, in the Note, in the Mortgage, or in any other Loan Document

d. All financial statements of Borrower and Guarantors, if any, are true and correct in all respects, fairly present the respective financial conditions of the subjects thereof, as of the respective dates thereof and no material adverse change has occurred that would affect Borrower's or Guarantors', if any, ability to repay the indebtedness evidenced by the Note and secured by the Mortgage

e. Borrower is duly formed, validly existing and in good standing under the laws of the State of _____ and has full power and authority to consummate the transactions contemplated under this Agreement.

4. Acknowledgements Borrower acknowledges that:

a. The Loan Documents are in full force and effect; and,

b. The principal balance of the loan as represented by the aforesaid Note as of the date of this Agreement is _____ DOLLARS ($_____) and principal and interest are unconditionally due and owing to the Lender as provided in the Note.

5. Costs Borrower shall pay all costs of the assumption made hereby, to include without limitation, attorneys' fees, and recording costs, as well as the cost of an endorsement to Lender's title insurance policy insuring the lien of the Mortgage after the recording of this Agreement. Such costs shall be due at closing hereunder and the payment thereof shall be a condition precedent to Lender's consent to the transfer of the Property to Borrower. In the event that it is determined additional costs relating to this transaction are due, Borrower agrees to pay such costs immediately upon demand.

6. Assumption Fee In consideration of Lender's consenting to the conveyance of the Property to the Borrower, Lender is entitled to, and has earned, an assumption fee in the amount of __ percent (___%) of the original principal face amount of the indebtedness evidenced by the Note. Said fee shall be due and payable upon the execution and delivery of this Agreement. Borrower hereby agrees and acknowledges that said fee is being charged solely for costs relating to the assumption of the Mortgage and not as interest for the forbearance or use of money.

7. Recordation The recording of this Agreement on the Public Records shall evidence the closing of the transaction described herein.

8. Paragraph Headings The paragraph headings used herein are for convenience of reference only and shall not be used in the interpretation or construction hereof.

9. Governing Law This Agreement shall be governed, interpreted, and construed by, through and under the laws of the State of _____.

7:9 Example Form - Mortgage Assumption Agreement Continued

10. **Time of the Essence** Time is of the essence of this Agreement.

11. **Attorneys' Fees** All costs incurred by Lender in enforcing this Agreement and in collection of sums due Lender from Borrower, to include, without limitation, reasonable attorneys' fees through all trials, appeals, and proceedings, to include, without limitation, any proceedings pursuant to the bankruptcy laws of the United States and any arbitration proceedings, shall be paid by Borrower.

12. **Binding Effect** This Agreement shall inure to the benefit of and be binding upon the parties hereto as well as their successors and assigns, heirs and personal representatives.

IN WITNESS WHEREOF, the parties hereto have duly executed this Agreement as follows:

As to Lender this ___ day of _____, 20_____

"LENDER"   WITNESSES:

_____   _____

As to Borrower this day of _____, 20_____

"BORROWER"   WITNESSES:

_____   _____

7:9 Example Form - Mortgage Assumption Agreement Continued

This form is included for example purposes only. The form is modified from the acceptable real estate forms as released by HUD. The services of a real estate professional should be retained to ensure the correct forms are used for your transaction.

EARNEST MONEY DEPOSIT

It is customary for a potential buyer to remit a certain amount of money upon making an offer to purchase a property. This money provides the seller with an assurance that the buyer is serious in their plans to purchase the property and provides the seller with a security in the event the potential buyer reneges on the agreement to purchase the property.

These funds are typically termed the earnest money deposit and these funds usually accompany the initial offer. If the offer is then accepted, the funds are typically held in "escrow" until the transaction has been finalized. If the buyer follows through with the transaction in accordance with the contract, the earnest money deposits are typically applied toward the costs to be paid by the buyer at the closing. If the transaction fails to reach completion and the reason for the failure is the fault of the seller or a flaw discovered with the property or title to the property, the earnest money deposit is typically refunded to the buyer. If the transaction fails to reach completion due to an action or inaction on the part of the buyer or a failure by the buyer to fulfill a point negotiated on the sales agreement, the earnest money funds are typically kept by the seller. These funds retained help to offset the costs incurred in the transaction and the selling time lost while the property was under contract to the buyer and therefore unable to be marketed for a valid sale.

It is important to document any and all funds that change hands during the transaction. This documentation of the transfer of funds protects both the buyer and the seller against future controversy, which may arise for a variance in the party's records. The careful documentation of the transfer of funds is also of assistance if the buyer intends to seek conventional financing at some point in the future. Many lenders are hesitant to accept simple private party receipts without third party verification. The best practice is to retain all cancelled checks and deposit statements in the file with written acknowledgement receipts.

Another valid reason for the use of an Earnest Money Deposit receipt is to outline the handling of the earnest money. In the following receipt the buyer acknowledges that they seller has the right to retain the deposited funds if they default on the purchase for any reason except clear title. This is an example form and you will want to consult a real estate attorney to ensure your earnest money receipt contains any acknowledgements, which may be applicable to your personal negotiation transaction.

Earnest money or deposit receipt

Received of _____ $_____ as earnest money, and in part payment for the purchase of the following described property situated in the County of _____ and State of _____ and known as _____, which we have this day sold and agreed to convey to _____ for $_____.

If adequate title to the premises is not good and cannot be made good within _____ days from this date, this agreement shall be void and the above earnest money deposit of $_____ shall be refunded. But if the title to the premises is now good, in the name of seller, or is made good in him within _____ days, and the purchaser refuses to accept the same, the earnest money deposit in the amount of $_____ shall be forfeited to _____. This forfeiture shall in no way affect the right of either party to enforce the specific performance of this contract.

Seller Signature: _____ Date: _____

I hereby agree to purchase the property for the price and upon the terms above mentioned, and agree to the conditions of forfeiture and all other conditions expressed.

Buyer Signature: _____ Date: _____

7:10 Example Form - Earnest Money Deposit Receipt
This form is included for example purposes only. The form is modified from the acceptable real estate forms as released by HUD. The services of a real estate professional should be retained to ensure the correct forms are used for your transaction.

DEED ESCROWS

In some states it may be allowed and even customary to escrow the deed, or put it in a hold account, rather than transfer and record the deed at the time of the sale of the property. This practice simplifies the requirements that the seller must take in order to obtain possession in the event of buyer default. Specific guidelines and practices for your state should be researched prior to utilizing a contract of this type. The handling of the deed may become another negotiation point between the buyer and the seller in the creative finance forum. The following sample shows some of the stipulations, which may be included in a deed escrow agreement. A real estate attorney or other competent professional will be able to provide specific details that are allowed in your State.

Contract to escrow deed by mortgagor of mortgaged premises

This agreement, dated _____, is between _____, hereinafter called seller, and _____, hereinafter called buyer, and _____, hereinafter called the escrow.

The seller is the owner of a certain tract of land situated in the county of _____, state of _____, commonly known as _____ the same being the land conveyed to seller by _____ on _____.

The seller is or is about to become the owner of certain mortgages aggregating the amount of $_____ which mortgages are described and designated as follows:

In order to save the seller the cost and expense of the foreclosing of the mortgages, in the event of default, or breach of the terms, seller has duly made, executed and delivered to the escrow certain good and sufficient fee simple deed of conveyance for the described premises to hold the deed in escrow to and for the uses and purposes set forth.

It is agreed as follows:

The seller now delivers to the escrow the deed for the above-described premises, which the escrow promises to hold and keep and to deliver to the buyer on _____, unless on or before that date the seller places on deposit with the escrow $_____ to the credit of the grantee (sum to be applied towards the payment of the mortgage debt), and upon deposit by the grantor the escrow will continue to hold and keep the deed until _____ and upon the last-mentioned date if the grantor has not before then paid to the grantee all sums due by reason of the mortgages, including principal and interest, according to the terms of the mortgages, and secured the proper receipts from the grantee, then the escrow shall convey the premises to grantee, who shall then be the sole and unconditional owner of the property and shall be entitled to the immediate possession of the property.

Grantee agrees that during the continuance of this agreement, until _____, that grantee shall not attempt a collection of all or any part of the sum due by reason of the mortgages nor disturb grantor in the possession of the premises, but on the last-mentioned date will accept the deed from escrow with all the rights and privileges conferred in full settlement of any and all sums due to by reason of the mortgage as principal and interest or otherwise; provided, however, that at any time prior to _____ grantor may pay the grantee the amount due by reason of the mortgages, in which event, and upon due proof to the escrow, the deed shall be returned and redelivered to the grantor.

7:11 Contract to Escrow Deed

Grantor agrees that upon default of the conditions of this contract, and upon presentation of the above-mentioned deed, to vacate and surrender the possession of the premises to grantee, who, then without suit or process, may enter and have exclusive possession of the premises.

Escrow accepts the deed in escrow and agrees to hold and keep the deed in accordance with the terms and conditions of this contract and for the uses and purposes set forth, and to deliver or redeliver the same upon the performance or nonperformance of the conditions set forth at length.

It is agreed between all the parties that all the terms, stipulations, and agreements contained in this contract shall be binding upon the parties and their heirs, executors, administrators, successors and assigns, as the case may be.

7:11 Contract to Escrow Deed Continued

This form is included for example purposes only. The form is modified from the acceptable real estate forms as released by HUD. The services of a real estate professional should be retained to ensure the correct forms are used for your transaction.

THE NOTE

If the buyer and the seller agree to a sale that requires the seller to hold a mortgage on the property it is common practice to draw up both a mortgage document and a promissory note.

A promissory note is a contract between the borrower and the lender. In the case of seller financing, the lender is actually the seller. Often simply referred to as a note, the document must contain certain key components to ensure it is legally binding and enforceable.

The note must be in writing.

The note must be between a borrower and a lender who have the ability to enter into a legally binding contract.

The note states the borrowers promise to pay a certain sum of money and the terms under which those monies will be paid.

The borrower signs the document and the completed note is given to the lender.

Promissory notes need not be complicated but they must clearly outline the terms under which the loan is being granted. Terms could include the principal amount of the mortgage, the interest rate agreed upon, the date payment is due, the late charge, if any, incurred when a payment is paid beyond the due date and the date which these late charges are assessed, the length of time payments shall be made, how the payments will be credited on the account for example to interest and then principal and any other details which have been negotiated between the buyer and the seller with regards to the repayment of the agreed to monies.

Simply put a promissory note is the written promise to repay a debt and acceptable terms and method for payment.

A promissory note can be obtained from a variety of sources including a competent real estate attorney. The following example incorporates all of the items listed and may be customized by your real estate attorney or other competent professional to suit your negotiated transaction.

Promissory Installment Note (w/Balloon Payment)

Date: _____ *(insert date)*

Borrower: _____ *(insert buyer(s) name)*

Borrower's Address: _____*(insert buyer's new address)*

Payee: _____*(insert seller(s) name)*

Place for Payment _____*(insert seller(s) mailing address)*

Principal Amount: $_____ *(insert total loan amount)* Term: _____ *(insert number of payments)*

Monthly Payments: $_____ *(insert total of payment)* _____*(insert number of months)*

1. INTEREST RATE

Annual interest rate on matured, unpaid amounts shall be _____% (_____) *(insert interest rate).*

2. PAYMENT TERMS

This Note is due and payable as follows, _____ (____) *(insert number of payments)* equal monthly payments of $_____ principal and interest *(insert monthly payment amount)*

The first such payment due and payable on the 1st day of _____ , 20____, and a like installment shall be due and payable on the same day of each succeeding month thereafter until the total principal of $_____ principal *(insert total principal amount)* is paid in full.

If each payment is not paid on time, the remaining balance will be subject to the maximum amount of interest permitted by the Laws of the State of _____. *(insert applicable State)*

3. BALLOON PAYMENT.

Borrower promises to make a single, final payment for the entire balance owed to the Payee on or before _____ *(due date for balloon payment).*

4. BORROWER'S PRE-PAYMENT RIGHT

Borrower reserves the right to prepay this Note in whole or in part, prior to maturity, without penalty.

5. PLACE FOR PAYMENT

Borrower promises to pay to the order of Payee at the place for payment and according to the terms for payment the principal amount plus interest at the rates stated above. All unpaid amounts shall be due by the final scheduled payment date.

6. DEFAULT AND ACCELERATION CLAUSE

If Borrower defaults in the payment of this Note or in the performance of any obligation, and the default continues after Payee gives Borrower notice of the default and the time within which it must be cured, as may be required by law or written agreement, then Payee may declare the unpaid principal balance and earned interest on this Note immediately due. Borrower and each surety, endorser, and guarantor waive all demands for payment, presentation for payment, notices of intentions to accelerate maturity, notices of acceleration of maturity, protests, and notices of protest, to the extent permitted by law.

7. INTEREST ON PAST DUE INSTALLMENTS AND CHARGES

All past due installments of principal and/or interest and/or all other past-due incurred charges shall bear interest after maturity at the maximum amount of interest permitted by the Laws of the Commonwealth of _____ until paid. Failure by Borrower to remit any payment by the 15th day following the date that such payment is due entitles the Payee hereof to declare the entire principal and accrued interest immediately due and payable. Payee's forbearance in enforcing a right or remedy, as set forth herein shall not be deemed a waiver of said right or remedy for a subsequent cause, breach or default of the Borrower's obligations herein.

8. INTEREST

Interest on this debt evidenced by this Note shall not exceed the maximum amount of non-usurious interest that may be contracted for, taken, reserved, charged, or received under law; any interest in excess of the maximum shall be credited on the principal of the debt or, if that has been paid, refunded. On any acceleration or required or permitted prepayment, any such excess shall be canceled automatically as of the acceleration or prepayment or, if already paid, credited on the principal of the debt, or, if the principal of the debt has been paid, refunded. This provision overrides other provisions in this instrument (and any other instruments) concerning this debt.

9. FORM OF PAYMENT

Any check, draft, Money Order, or other instrument given in payment of all or any portion hereof may be accepted by the holder and handled in collection in the customary manner, but the same shall not constitute payment hereunder or diminish any rights of the holder hereof except to the extent that actual cash proceeds of such instruments are unconditionally received by the payee and applied to this indebtedness in the manner elsewhere herein provided.

10. ATTORNEY'S FEES

If this Note is given to an attorney for collection or enforcement, or if suit is brought for collection or enforcement, or if it is collected or enforced through probate, bankruptcy, or other judicial proceeding, then Borrower shall pay Payee all costs of collection and enforcement, including reasonable attorney's fees and court costs in addition to other amounts due.

11. SEVERABILITY

If any provision of this Note or the application thereof shall, for any reason and to any extent, be invalid or unenforceable, neither the remainder of this Note nor the application of the provision to other persons, entities or circumstances shall be affected thereby, but instead shall be enforced to the maximum extent permitted by law.

12. BINDING EFFECT

The covenants, obligations and conditions herein contained shall be binding on and inure to the benefit of the heirs, legal representatives, and assigns of the parties hereto.

13. DESCRIPTIVE HEADINGS

The descriptive headings used herein are for convenience of reference only and they are not intended to have any effect whatsoever in determining the rights or obligations under this Note.

14. CONSTRUCTION

The pronouns used herein shall include, where appropriate, either gender or both, singular and plural.

15. GOVERNING LAW

This Note shall be governed, construed, and interpreted by, through and under the Laws of the Commonwealth of _____.
Borrower is responsible for all obligations represented by this Note.

EXECUTED this _____ day of _____, 20_____

Borrower's Signature: _____

Borrower's Printed or Typed Name: _____

7:12 Example Form – Promissory Note with Balloon Payment

This form is included for example purposes only. The form is modified from the acceptable real estate forms as released by HUD. The services of a real estate professional should be retained to ensure the correct forms are used for your transaction.

PROMISORY NOTE SECURED BY MORTGAGE
(short form with explanatory key)

In the City of _____, State of _____ on this date _____,
_____ in the year _____ for value received, I promise to pay to
_____ at _____ the sum of
_____ dollars, with interest of _____ per annum accumulated on any unpaid principal.

These payments shall begin _____, _____ and be due the ___ day of each month and continuing until said principal and interest have been repaid. Monthly payments in the amount of _____ shall constitute principal and interest payments.

This note may be prepaid in whole or in part at any time without prepayment penalty.

There shall be a ____ day grace period for each monthly payment. A late fee of _____ shall be added to each payment made after its grace period has expired.

Each payment shall be credited first to the accumulated interest then due and the remainder on principal. Unpaid interest shall bear interest like the principal.

Should default be made in payment of any installment when due, the entire principal and accrued interest shall immediately become due at the option of the holder of the note.

If legal action is necessary to collect this note, I promise to pay such sums as the court may fix.

This note is secured by a mortgage bearing the same date as this note and made in favor of

---

7:13 Sample Form Promissory Note Secured by Mortgage

This form is included for example purposes only. The form is modified from the acceptable real estate forms as released by HUD. The services of a real estate professional should be retained to ensure the correct forms are used for your transaction.

The components of the example promissory note allow certain rights to be legally enforced on the part of both the buyer and the seller. This promissory note is explained as follows:

- State that the document is a promissory note.

- Give the location and the date of the notes signing. As with any contract, the location stated in the contract establishes which state laws govern the execution of the document.

- State that the borrower has received something of value and in return, promises to pay the debt as described in the note.

- Identify who is to receive the payments.

- Show where the borrower is to send or make said payments.

- Show the amount of funds for which the note is being signed

- Show the interest rate on the debt.

- State the date from which interest will be charged and payments shall begin.

- Show the amount of the payments to be made including principal and interest.

- State the prepayment decision. Prepayment of all or part of the loan funds prior to a specified date is sometimes penalized as part of the negotiation process. Prepayment penalty regulations vary by state and if a prepayment penalty is to be imposed on a loan, the applicable laws should be fully researched.

- Indicate the grace period, if any that is allowed prior to the addition of a late-charge to the payment.

- Clarify exactly how the payments remitted shall be applied. In this instance, all payments are applied first to the interest currently accumulated with the remainder of the payment applied to the principal balance owing on the loan.

- Provide the lender with the right to accelerate the loan and demand immediate payment of all interest and principal owed if the borrower misses any individual payments. This clause allows the acceleration to be at the lender decision.

- Causes the borrower to agree to pay any costs incurred by the lender if the borrower falls behind on the payments agreed upon

- The promissory note is tied to the mortgage that secures it making this a mortgage loan. Without this reference, the note would be a personal loan.

The borrower signs the note and is sometimes referred to as the note maker. If two or more persons sign the note, it is common to include a statement in the note that h borrowers are jointly and severally making the note. This means that the terms of the note and the obligations created are enforceable on the makers as a group or upon each note maker individually.

THE MORTGAGE

Financing transactions that contain real estate are typically secured in the form of a mortgage.

A mortgage causes the note to be secured against real property rather than other property or as an unsecured personal loan. Typically, a seller will utilize both a note and a mortgage in these types of financing situations. The note is the promise to repay the funds while a mortgage is a separate agreement from the note and provides the security or collateral in the event of non-payment.

The key components of a mortgage include the act of putting the property as collateral and the conditions under which the buyer will maintain the collateral to protect the interest of the lender while the note is payable.

The following page contains an example of a simplified mortgage. This example will illustrate all of the basic requirements needed to create a legally binding document. It is recommended that the services of a real estate professional or competent attorney be retained to create and customize the mortgage document needed for your scenario.

MORTGAGE

This mortgage made this _____ day of _____ between _____ hereinafter called Mortgagor, and _____ hereinafter called Mortgagee.

Whereas, the Mortgagor is indebted to the Mortgagee in the principal sum of _____ dollars payable _____ as evidenced by the Mortgagor's note of the same date as this mortgage, hereinafter called Note.

To secure the Mortgagee the repayment of the indebtedness evidenced by said Note, with interest thereon, the Mortgagor does hereby mortgage, grant, and convey to the Mortgagee the following described property in the County of _____ State of _____.

Lot ___, Block _____, as shown on Page _____ of Deed Book _____ filed with the County Recorder of said County and State.

7:13 Sample Form Mortgage

Furthermore, the Mortgagor fully warrants the title to said land and will defend the same against the lawful claims of all persons.

If the Mortgagor, his heirs, legal representatives or assigns pay unto the Mortgagee, all sums due by said Note then this mortgage and the estate created shall hereby cease and be null and void.

Until said note is fully paid, the Mortgagor agrees to pay all taxes on said land and the Mortgagor agrees not to remove or demolish building or other improvements on the mortgaged land without the approval of the Mortgagee.

The mortgagor agrees to carry adequate homeowners insurance to protect the Mortgagee in the event of damage or destruction of the mortgaged property.

The Mortgagor agrees to keep the mortgaged property in good repair and not permit waste or deterioration of the property.

It is further agreed that the Mortgagee shall have the right to inspect the mortgaged property as may be necessary for the security of the Note.

If the Mortgagor does not abide by this Mortgage or the accompanying Note, the Mortgagee may declare the entire unpaid balance on the Note immediately due and payable.

If the Mortgagor sells or otherwise conveys title to the mortgaged property, the Mortgagee may declare the entire unpaid balance on the Note immediately due and payable.

If all or part of the Mortgaged property is taken by act of eminent domain, any sums of money received shall be applied to the Note.

In WITNESS WHEROF, the Mortgagor has executed this mortgage.

_____
Mortgagor

7:13 Sample Mortgage Continued
This form is included for example purposes only. The form is modified from the acceptable real estate forms as released by HUD. The services of a real estate professional should be retained to ensure the correct forms are used for your transaction.

Mortgage Key

The first item on a mortgage is the date of its making and the names of the parties involved. Mortgagor is the person who owes the mortgage and a Mortgagee is the person who is receiving the payments or the lender.

- The debt for which the mortgage is being held as collateral is named.

- The borrower of the funds conveys the property being held as collateral to the lender.

- The mortgaged property is then described.

- The borrower states that the property being provided as collateral legally belongs to them and that the borrower will be responsible for defending ownership against all other claims of interest by other properties. The seller or lender will want to verify this claim by the buyer through a title search and, at times, require the buyer to carry title insurance as a combat against any future claims to the title by other parties.

- This is known as the defeasance clause and it contains provisions to nullify and make void the mortgage when the note has been paid in full.

- The borrower makes certain promises to the lender that protect the collateral or property, which acts as security for the loan.

  Covenant to pay taxes is the borrowers agreement to pay the property taxes on the mortgaged property. This is an important factor for the lender because if the taxes are not paid they may create a lien on the property, which is superior to the lien held by the lender.

  Covenant against removal prohibits the borrower from removing or demolishing any building or improvement on the property. Demolishing or removing improvements may reduce the value of the collateral offered to the lender against the note.

  Covenant of insurance requires the borrower to carry adequate homeowners insurance to protect the lender interest in the collateral in the event of the damage or destruction of a part of the property.

  Covenant of good repair requires that the borrower keep the collateral in good condition. This is also sometimes referred to as the covenant of preservation and maintenance.

Provides the lender with the right to inspect the property to ensure it is being maintained in a manner, which protects the value of the collateral given to the lender.

This is referred to as an acceleration clause. The acceleration clause permits the lender to demand all monies owed as payable immediately. If the borrower cannot pay the money owed in full, a foreclosure proceeding is implemented and the property is sold with the lender receiving monies from the sale to pay the funds owed. This clause is used if the borrower breaks any clause included in the agreement.

This clause is referred to as the alienation clause or due-on-sale clause. It allows the lender to call the entire loan balance as due if the property is sold or conveyed by the borrower to another individual.

If any part of all of the property is taken by the act of eminent domain this clause provides the lender with the right to receive any money paid as part of the action to offset the balance of the loan owed.

This section is a formality that states the borrower has created this mortgage. The signature of the borrower fulfills the same requirement.

The borrower acknowledges the mortgage by the signing of the document. In some states, an authorized person such as a notary public or an officer of the court must witness this signature.

When a note or loan is paid in full, the lender will typically return the promissory note to the borrower. The lender will also provide the borrower with a satisfaction of mortgage document that states the promissory note has been paid in full. This allows the mortgage to be discharged from the public records. It is important that this document be recorded by the public recorder in the same county in which the original mortgage document was recorded.

8

CHAPTER

Buyer Analysis

It is important for both potential sellers and potential buyers to understand the aspects of a borrower's profile that can affect the probability of a borrower to repay a loan. These aspects include items such as

- past credit history

- debt load in relationship to income

- employment history

- and many other factors

The following pages are designed to provide both the buyer and the seller with information regarding the methods and theories utilized in the conventional mortgage market to approve or decline a loan. This material is important knowledge when entering into a seller-financing scenario as it provides a better understanding of the reason a buyer desires financing outside of the conventional mortgage arena as well as providing the seller with knowledge on how to assess a potential buyer.

It is important to remember that buyers and sellers are entering a creative finance negotiation for a variety of reasons, the most important being that the "normal" or standard methods of buying and selling are not available to the parties. The guidelines set by the lenders for both property qualification and borrower qualification can be very strict. In the case of a private transaction, each of the guidelines is actually a point of negotiation.

Before beginning to profile a potential buyer, some basic information will be needed. The form on the following page is a useful tool for both the buyer and the seller. The form allows the buyer to prepare for the negotiating meeting having all of the needed information and documentation, which may be needed, readily available. The form provides the seller with a simplified format that will allow them to obtain all of the information they require for basic profiling of the buyer in one quick conversation.

Pre-Qualification Questionnaire Date: _____

Referral: _____ Phone: _____

Borrower Name: _____ Co-Borrower Name: _____

Home Phone: _____ Other Phone: _____ Best time(s) to call: _____

DOB: _____ SSN: _____ DOB: _____ SSN: _____

May I run a credit report?___ Yes ___ No   May I run a credit report? ___ Yes ___ No

Employer: _____ Employer: _____

Address: _____ Address: _____

Phone: _____ No yrs. ___ Position: _____ Phone: _____ No yrs. ___ Position: _____

Current Address: _____ Check? ___ Yes ___ No

Landlord/Mortgage Holder: _____ Phone: _____

Rent ____ Own ___ No. Yrs: ___ Have you chosen a home to purchase? ___ Yes ___ No Value$ _____

___ 1st ___2nd ___Rate/Term Refi ___ C/O Refi ___ Special: _____

Gross Income   Debt
Borrowers Mthly $_____   Mortgage/Rental Payment $_____
        Prev Year $_____   Auto Payment $_____
Co-Borrowers Mthly $_____   Auto Payment #2 $_____
        Prev Year $_____   Installment Debt / Type ___ $_____
Other Income _____ $_____   Installment Debt / Type ___ $_____
Other Income _____ $_____   Other _____ $_____
        Total Income $_____   Total Debt $_____
                          DTI _____%

Explanation of Credit Situation/Notes: _____
_____
_____
_____

Outcome: _____

8:1 Sample Form Prequalification Questionnaire
This form is included for example purposes only. The services of a real estate professional should be retained to ensure the correct forms are used for your transaction.

Pre-qualification questionnaire key

Date	You will always want to date the query.	The date allows for a quick assessment of how current the information contained in the form.
Borrower Name	You will need the borrower's full name including middle initial and any additional information Jr., Sr., II. Do not use nicknames, however please note any aliases that the borrower commonly uses.	Names, especially among family, can be very similar. The more identifying information you can acquire the more pure your credit report will be.
Co-Borrower Name	It is important to acquire correct identifying information for this person as it is for your borrower.	
Date of Birth/Social Security Number	This information is vital when you are pulling a credit report.	
May I run a credit report?	It is imperative that you ask this question. You are not allowed to run a credit report on any individual without their prior consent.	
Employer	This information aids you in determining some of the issues that may arise during the course of the loan.	A person's stability of past employment is at times an indicator of their future ability to maintain employment and therefore make loan payments as agreed.
Number of years at present employment	You will typically want a minimum of two years employment history.	A two-year history is often a sufficient indicator of a person's ability to maintain employment income.
Current Address	This is identifying information you will want to have to clarify identity on the credit report.	

Landlord/Mortgage Holder	A potential buyer's performance with a previous landlord or mortgage holder is a strong indication of their probable performance in your transaction.	
Number of years?	You will often want to obtain a two year residence history on your potential buyer	Residence history is an indicator of the potential buyer's stability and can help predict their performance should the sale follow through to completion.
Income Information	In order to pre-qualify a potential buyer you must have complete income information. Debt ratio's are explained later in this section and can affect a buyer's ability to pay their mortgage as agreed.	
Debt Information	Debt load will be visible on the Credit Report but it is important to ask a potential buyer this information.	There may be new debt, which is not yet showing on the report but may crop up prior to closing the loan. Additionally child support payments do affect the debt load.
Explanation of credit situation?	This is the opportunity for notes. Your buyers will usually explain any information that is present on their credit report.	Gathering this information now allows you to pre-plan the negotiation meeting, request any additional documentation that you may need and is an excellent reference if problems appear later in the loan process.

Understanding Credit Reports

In creative financing, it is important that both the buyer and the seller understand the credit report and the potential impact the information contained on the report may have on the outcome of the transaction.

Every action a consumer takes effects their credit report. These actions can have a negative or a positive effect.

Credit reports are an overview of a person's entire history of spending and payment habits. Almost everything that we do financially is reported, collected, and stored in each person's credit profile. The primary concern of a seller is any action that had a negative or derogatory impact on a buyer's credit history.

Debt: The term describing any situation in which funds are borrowed.

Debt Load: The amount of debt an individual is carrying (owes).

Debt load may include many items. The most common being:

> Credit card debt
> Department store debt
> Charge accounts
> Auto loans
> Student loans
> Mortgages

The ability to borrow more money or to have additional credit extended is effected by how much debt a potential borrower currently carries.

As a seller, you will be concerned with debt-to-income ratio.

Debt-to-Income Ratio's: The amount of open debt weighed against the borrower's monthly income.

The higher the DTI the greater the potential risk of a borrower default on the loan.

The credit report will provide a relatively accurate view of current debt load. The seller should document income for comparison purposes.

Late payments: Any payments that have been paid more than 30 days past the due date

Late payments can be a severe blemish on the credit report.

A late payment will appear on the credit report for two years, though credit bureaus may keep them in the credit file for up to seven years.

Bankruptcy: Bankruptcy can remain on the credit report for as long as 10 years.

A borrower in the prime market may have to wait up to four years to attempt to qualify for most prime loans and must re-establish a credit history during that time. This re-establishment of credit will aid in showing that the borrower is no longer a credit risk.

The sub-prime market is more lenient as to time that must elapse before obtaining mortgage finance. The sub-prime market is also more lenient concerning the amount credit the borrower must establish before seeking mortgage financing. The sub-prime market gains their security in the borrower through higher interest rates and fees.

Collection accounts: Accounts that a borrower fails to pay as agreed.

These accounts are turned over to a collection department or agency in the attempt to collect the payments owed. The initial creditor and the collection agencies report these accounts to the bureaus.

If your borrower has paid these debts in full, have them obtain a letter stating that the debt has been completely satisfied and no further action on their part or the creditor is necessary.

Medical collections: Accounts to medical service providers that the borrower has failed to pay.

Medical Collection Accounts are often treated differently than other collection accounts.

You will need to consider the type of collection accounts in the profile.

Credit inquiries: Accesses to a borrower's credit profile.

These inquiries are visible on the credit report.

A credit-gathering spree means that the borrower is out to expand their credit quickly for a specific purchase.

A series of inquiries could also indicate that new credit obligations are present but not visible on the report.

Credit Bureau Scores: Scores generated based solely on credit bureau data.

Credit Bureau Scores are one of the many elements that are reshaping today's mortgage industry.

Credit scoring has been around since the 1950's and Credit Bureau Scores became widely available in the 1980's.

Credit Scores are now used extensively in such industries as mortgage lending, auto lending, and bankcards.

Credit Bureau Score: Credit Bureau scoring is a scientific way of assessing how **(CBS)** likely a borrower is to pay back a loan.

How is the CBS calculated?

A Credit Bureau Score is based on the data available in the borrower's credit report.

The score measures the relative degree of risk a potential borrower represents to the lender or investor.

A credit bureau score is not a measure of a borrower's income, assets, or bank account. These factors are taken into consideration by lenders and investors independent of credit scores.

Score Range: Fair, Isaac Credit Bureau Scores range from approximately 450 to 850 points.

Repositories: Credit scores are available through three national repositories.

The scoring programs of these credit bureaus are called:

BEACON	at EQUIFAX (CBI)
EMPIRICA	at TRANS UNION
TRW/FAIR, ISAAC	at TRW

This score is calculated at the repository and is based on the data within that repositories credit file.

FICO: A Fair, Isaac Credit Bureau Score, sometimes referred to as a FICO score is calculated using a system of scorecards.

In developing these scorecards, Fair, Isaac uses actual credit data from millions of consumers. They apply complex mathematical methods to perform extensive research into credit patterns that forecast credit performance.

Through this process, Fair, Isaac identifies distinctive credit patterns. Each pattern corresponds to a likelihood that a consumer will make his or her loan payments as agreed.

This score is based on all the credit-related data in the credit bureau report – not just negative data such as a missed mortgage payment or bankruptcies.

Score Data: The types of credit information used in the credit bureau scorecards are typically the same items seller will use to make a credit decision. These can include:

Payment history
Public records and collection items
Severity, recentness, and frequency of delinquencies noted in the trade line section
Outstanding Debt
Number of balances recently reported
Average balance across all trade lines
Relationship between total balances and total credit limits on revolving trade lines
Credit History
Age of oldest trade line
Inquiries and new account openings
Number of inquiries in the last year
Number of new accounts opened in the last year
Amount of time since most recent inquiry
Types of credit in use
Number of trade lines for each type:
Bankcard
Travel and Entertainment cards
Department store cards
Personal finance company references

Installment loans
Other credit

Fair, Isaac observes tens of thousands of credit report histories of mortgage borrowers to determine which credit report items or combination of items are the most predictive of future risk. This data indicates the amount of weight each item should contribute to a credit decision.

FAIR, ISAAC CREDIT BUREAU SCORES DO NOT USE RACE, COLOR, RELIGION, NATIONAL ORIGIN, SEX, MARITAL STATUS, OR AGE AS PREDICTIVE CHARACTERISTICS.

OCCUPATION AND LENGTH OF TIME IN PRESENT HOUSING ARE ALSO NOT USED IN THE SCORECARDS.

ANY INFORMATION THAT IS NOT PRESENT IN THE CREDIT FILE IS NOT USED IN CREATING A CREDIT BUREAU SCORECARD.

Understanding a score's impact

A Fair, Isaac Credit Bureau Score is a means of rank-ordering potential borrowers based on the likelihood that they will pay their credit obligations as agreed.

A higher score indicates a better credit quality. If all other things are equal, borrowers with a score of 640 are less likely to default on a loan than borrowers with a score of 560.

The Fair, Isaac Credit Bureau Score models at each credit repository is of similar design and the scores are scaled to indicate a similar level of risk across all three repositories. In other words, a score of 660 at one bureau will represent a similar level of risk as a score of 660 at another bureau.

The risk is defined in terms of the number of accounts that remain in good standing compared to those that default.

Sample credit score ranges for new mortgage borrowers from a national sample	
Score Range	Number of good loans for each bad loan showing delinquency or foreclosure (# of good to 1 bad)
Below 600	8 to 1
700 – 719	123 to 1
Above 800	1,292 to 1

Credit Bureau Scores will rank-order potential borrowers based on risk or the number of good loans to bad loans denoted by a score. This rank ordering is likely to fluctuate due to changes in the economy, regional differences, changes in product offerings or other reasons.

A lender using credit scores will compare performance of their loans by score over time to determine the relationship of score and performance for their own market environment.

Report Appearance

Credit reports can take multiple visual forms depending on the bureau that issued the report and the type of record being requested. Regardless of the initial visual variations, all credit reports contain the same basic elements. These include borrower details and data, a summary of all of the credit inclusions, and a detailed breakdown of the borrower's current and historical credit transactions.

The upper portion of credit report will typically include identifying information including your name or company name as the individual, who requested the report.

Report type will usually be included in the header. Report type may be individual or joint.

Information relating to the individual within the credit bureau who pulled the report and the internal case ID # assigned to the report will be defined in the header of the report. This information will be important if you must request updates to the report or address a discrepancy in the report with the credit bureau.

MERGED INFILE CREDIT REPORT

Prepared For:	Property Address:	Prepared By:	Date Rec:
Attention:	Loan Type: Purpose of Loan: Report Type:	Computer ID: Lender Case #:	Date Comp: Date Revised:

APPLICANT

Name:
SSN: DOB:
Marital Status: Dependents:
:
Home Phone:

Present Address:

Since: Own / Rent

Previous Address:

From: To: Own / Rent

CO-APPLICANT

Name:
SSN: DOB:
Marital Status: Dependents:
:
Home Phone:

Present Address:

Since: Own / Rent

Previous Address:

From: To: Own / Rent

Date data will be included within the report. Date data can include the date the request was received by the credit bureau, the date the credit bureau completed the report, and the date of any revisions created by the credit bureau in relationship to the report.

Date is important because underwriting typically stipulates that the report must be current, or within a certain date range, in order to be used for closing.

If the report is out of date, underwriting will request a new report in order to ensure that no changes have occurred in the borrower's credit profile during the processing stage of the loan. You should caution your borrower not to make any large purchases or take any action that may alter the contents of the report until after the loan has closed.

Borrower Information

The credit report will contain details relating to the individual or individuals to whom the credit report applies.

This portion includes specifics such as full name, social security number, and date of birth. Information relating to the borrowers address and employment may be included in this segment of the report. It is important that you remember that information you have gained directly from the borrower may be more up-to-date than information contained within the credit report.

Variations in borrower address and employment are common within the report. You should note any discrepancy between the report and your file information and verify with the potential borrower to ensure that the report does not contain entries that relate to another individual with a similar name. If you note a discrepancy, you must address these differences before the package is submitted to underwriting.

MERGED INFILE CREDIT REPORT

Prepared For:	Property Address:	Prepared By:	Date Rec:
Attention:	Loan Type: Purpose of Loan: Report Type:	Computer ID: Lender Case #:	Date Comp: Date Revised:

APPLICANT	CO-APPLICANT
Name: SSN: DOB: Marital Status: Dependents:: Home Phone: Present Address: Since: Own / Rent Previous Address: From: To: Own / Rent	Name: SSN: DOB: Marital Status: Dependents: Home Phone: Present Address: Since: Own / Rent Previous Address: From: To: Own / Rent

Borrower and Co-Borrower identifying information is entered in this section.

You should verify that all details entered match the information included on the loss mitigation summary.

KENNEY

Credit Summary

The credit report will contain a segment that summarizes the details contained within the actual report. You should review this area to ensure that the inclusions do not bring to mind a red flag issue. You may need to question the homeowner more closely regarding these matters.

CREDIT SUMMARY

	PAYMENTS	BALANCES	LIMITS	TRADES	30+	60+	90+
REVOLVING	0	2061	2200	4	4	4	17
INSTALLMENT 1307	1307	79365	90610	25	34	8	27
REAL ESTATE	378	35384	36600	1	2	0	0
OPEN/OTHER	991	1041	1041	5	0	0	0
TOTAL	2676	117851	129451	38	40	12	44

INQUIRIES 50   # PUBLIC RECORDS 0   # BANKRUPTCIES 0
WORST TRADE 9   OLDEST DATE 07/01/89   # SATISFACTORIES 17

The summary will contain details identifying the types of credit that the borrower has available. You wish to ensure that the types and amount of credit available to the homeowner is exported into the DTI Analysis Form.

If you are using a system that does not automatically export report data into the Analysis Forms, you will need to enter each credit account, payment, and status by hand.

Credit payment totals and current balances will appear within the credit summary portion of your report.

You will confirm the payment information when you review the report inclusions.

Then you will use this information to confirm the debt ratio information and begin isolating potential loss mitigation options for the homeowner.

A summary data analysis of the details of the report will be included within the summary. This analysis will assist you in completing the scoring key. Much of the data you will use during credit scoring and mitigation screening will be summarized with in this section. Before you export the data into the credit-scoring key, debt-to-income ratio form, or loss mitigation application, you must review the report with the homeowner to ensure that all of the inclusions of the summary are correct and relate to active accounts. You will confirm the status of each account by reviewing the detail pages of the credit report.

CREDIT SUMMARY

	PAYMENTS	BALANCES	LIMITS	TRADES	30+	60+	90+
REVOLVING	0	2061	2200	4	4	4	17
INSTALLMENT 1307	1307	79365	90610	25	34	8	27
REAL ESTATE	378	35384	36600	1	2	0	0
OPEN/OTHER	991	1041	1041	5	0	0	0
TOTAL	2676	117851	129451	38	40	12	44

INQUIRIES   50   # PUBLIC RECORDS   0   # BANKRUPTCIES   0
WORST TRADE 9   OLDEST DATE   07/01/89   # SATISFACTORIES   17

The number of inquiries into credit profile will be totaled and entered into the summary.

A detailed breakdown of the companies that made credit inquiries will be included at the end of the report.

The homeowner may be required to provide an explanation for any excessive inquiries.

Credit inquiries may indicate that the homeowner has already attempted to remedy the delinquency through outside measures, such as a refinance.

You should review the data relating to these inquiries and discuss the results of any outside efforts the homeowner has made.

Specifics regarding public records, bankruptcy, and the worst trade payment history that you will encounter in the report will be included within the credit summary.

You should note these entries to ensure that you locate the applicable data within the report relating to any bankruptcy, late payment, or public record detailed within the summary.

Public records could relate to liens placed against the property not related to a mortgage or refinance. These liens could become a factor in loss mitigation negotiations where the surrender of the property is being considered.

If a judgment or public record exists in the borrower profile, the details of that record will be included within the report.

This data could include bankruptcy or foreclosure actions as well as judgments and other public records.

CREDIT SUMMARY

	PAYMENTS	BALANCES	LIMITS	TRADES	30+	60+	90+
REVOLVING	0	2061	2200	4	4	4	17
INSTALLMENT 1307	1307	79365	90610	25	34	8	27
REAL ESTATE	378	35384	36600	1	2	0	0
OPEN/OTHER	991	1041	1041	5	0	0	0
TOTAL	2676	117851	129451	38	40	12	44

# INQUIRIES 50	# PUBLIC RECORDS 0	# BANKRUPTCIES 0
WORST TRADE 9	OLDEST DATE 07/01/89	# SATISFACTORIES 17

The oldest date field indicates the date that the borrower fist obtained credit.

This inclusion allows you to ensure that an adequate credit history is available to the borrower. Many underwriting guidelines will require the potential borrower have at least a two-year credit history with at least three open active trade lines. If your potential borrower does not have a sufficient credit history or quantity of accounts, you may need to take alternative actions to aid the borrower in creating a credit profile that meets the minimum requirements of the loan guidelines.

It is important to address any issues early in the prequalification process. Proactively addressing issues early in the process helps to minimize stipulation requests, speeds the loan process, and facilitates positive relationships with borrowers, referral partners, and affinity service providers. This positive relationship building activity helps to ensure that your office gains the reputation as the office that can get the job done.

If a judgment or public record exists in the borrower profile, the details of that record will be included within the report.

This data could include bankruptcy or foreclosure actions as well as judgments and other public records.

You should scrutinize any inclusion within this section thoroughly to determine the status of the public record, the age of the public record, and the manner that the record will affect your borrower's approval status.

The type of public record will be named.

This typing will indicate to you the specific handling of the matter per the loss mitigation option that is being considered for the homeowner.

The report will include the dates pertaining to the specific public record.

The opened date will indicate the age of the judgment.

The last active date may affect the handling of the record depending upon the specific loss mitigation option being considered for the homeowner.

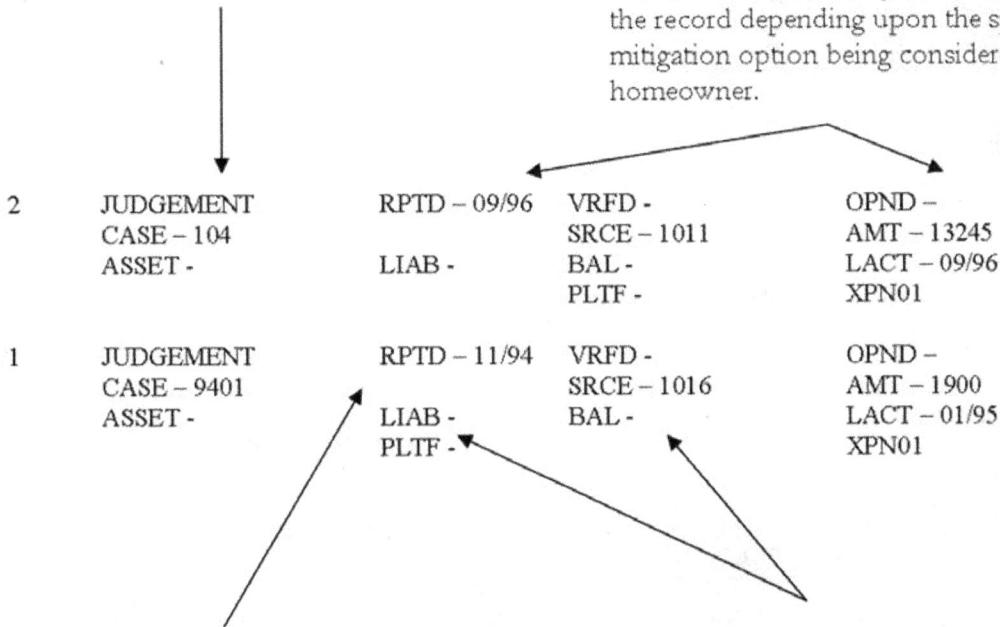

2	JUDGEMENT	RPTD – 09/96	VRFD -	OPND –
	CASE – 104		SRCE – 1011	AMT – 13245
	ASSET -	LIAB -	BAL -	LACT – 09/96
			PLTF -	XPN01

1	JUDGEMENT	RPTD – 11/94	VRFD -	OPND –
	CASE – 9401		SRCE – 1016	AMT – 1900
	ASSET -	LIAB -	BAL -	LACT – 01/95
		PLTF -		XPN01

Data regarding the status of the record will be included.

A satisfied judgment or closed bankruptcy will affect your file differently than an open or active record.

The liability or balance of the record will be included.

You will want to verify these figures and compare them to the specific
Underwriting Guidelines of the chosen loan program.

Underwriting guidelines will vary regarding the age requirements of a public record.

Score Factors

The name of the repository issuing the credit score included with the report will be included.

The lender negotiating the loss mitigation workout will designate the repository score that will be used for the process.

This designation is a result of regional

The code of the applicable agency will be entered to confirm the source of the score.

EFX = Equifax

8   BEACON SCORE   EFX01
     519
     SERIOUS DELINQUENCY AND DEROGATORY PUBLIC RECORD OR COLLECTION FILED
     AMOUNT OWED ON DELINQUENT ACCOUNTS
     PROPORTION OF BALANCES TO CREDIT LIMITS TOO HIGH ON REVOLVING ACCOUNTS
     LENGTH OF TIME ACCOUNTS HAVE BEEN ESTABLISHED

8   EMPIRICA SCORE   TRU01
     493
     SERIOUS DELINQUENCY, AND PUBLIC RECORD OR COLLECTION FILED
     LEVEL OF DELINQUENCY ON ACCOUNTS
     TIME SINCE DELINQUENCY IS TOO RECENT OR UNKNOWN
     PROPORTION OF REVOLVING BALANCES TO REVOLVING CREDIT LIMITS IS TOO HIGH

8   FAIR ISAAC SCORE   XPN01
     529
     SERIOUS DELINQUENCY AND PUBLIC RECORD OR COLLECTION FILED
     PROPORTION OF BALANCES TOO HIGH ON REVOLVING ACCOUNTS
     NUMBER OF ACCOUNTS DELINQUENT
     LENGTH OF TIME SINCE LEGAL ITEM FILED OR COLLECTION ITEM REPORTED

The factors that affect the score will be included on the report. This information is often referred to by a score factor code.

Score Factors – Reason Codes

To understand why a credit report scored the way it did, you must review the reason codes given within each score. These reason codes provide the top reasons why a profile did not score higher. These scores are only the top reasons and other factors probably contribute to the overall score. You should review both the score and the reasons the score ranks where it does.

To find the scores reason code you should locate a number or a letter followed by a brief description.

For example, a score of 540 may have the following factors:

02 – Delinquency on accounts
01 – Amount owed on accounts is too high
09 – Too many accounts opened in the last 12 months
19 – Too few accounts currently paid as agreed

Score factors are less meaningful for higher scoring credit records as they merely point to the reasons why a very good credit report was not perfect.

Examples of adverse factors that may appear on the report as a consideration in the score calculation are:

Current outstanding balances on accounts
Delinquency report on accounts
Accounts not paid as agreed
Too few open accounts
Too many open accounts
Too many bank accounts with outstanding balances
Too many finance company accounts
Payment history too new to rate
Number of inquiries within the last 12 months
Number of accounts opened within the last 12 months
Balance too high
Length of credit history
No recent account information
Too few accounts rate as current
Amount past due on accounts
No adverse factors
Recent derogatory public record or collection

This is not an all-inclusive listing. The items listed are examples of issues you may find in the score coding section of a report. You should review each report carefully to determine the factors specific to that credit profile.

Fraud Alert

The fraud alert field is becoming increasingly filled field within today's environment. Any data that indicates possible fraud activity will be included with in this section. The information will often become a warning entry because of some action taken by the borrower but any entry other than *"available and clear"* should be reviewed and discussed with the potential borrower.

Basic information noted by the credit bureau as potential fraud will be flagged.

If the entry is not related to an action taken by the borrower, the borrower may be a victim of identity theft and all entries in the body of the report should be scrutinized to ensure that all of the accounts do belong to the borrower.

An example of a fraud alert entry would be the number of inquiries in the last 60 days.

Excessive inquiries may be a result of the mortgage shopping process. In this case, there is little cause for concern as the alert is related to an action taken by your borrower. However, excessive inquiries could indicate access to the credit profile by another party who is seeking to open fraudulent accounts in your borrower's name.

FRAUD ALERT

1	TRANS ALERT # INQUIRIES IN LAST 60 DAYS: 04 RECORDED INQUIRIES ALTER	TRU01
1	HAWK ALERT HAWK AVAILABLE AND CLEAR	TRU 01

Details regarding any activity that may indicate fraud will be included.

AVAILABLE AND CLEAR =   No information found

inquiries in the last 60 days =   potential credit gathering spree.

At times, this could indicate a stolen profile but more often, this insert is related to the search current loan search.

CREDIT HISTORY DETAILS

The main body of the report will contain details of each account contained within the borrower's credit history. You will wish to scrutinize each entry within this section to determine the status of the borrower's credit, gain an understanding of the borrower payment and spending habits, and complete the credit history-scoring key.

The credit history-scoring key will be explained later and is included within the appendix section of your workbook. This key will assist you in extracting the necessary details from the credit profile.

CREDIT HISTORY

E C O A	CREDITOR ACCOUNT NO	DATE RPTED	DATE LAST ACT	DATE OPND	LIMIT / HIGHEST CREDIT	PRESENT STATUS		TERMS	PAY AMT	TYPE AND ACCT STATUS	HISTORICAL STATUS			
						BALANCE OWING	AMOUNT PAST DUE				NO MOS HIIST REV	3 0	60	9 0
8	AFM-BLOOM #APRINTLO COLLECTION	02/99	04/94		425	425				OPN05				

The name of the creditor and the account number will be included within the report.

Account numbers are often shortened on the credit report and the full account number may not appear. You can obtain the full account number directly from your borrower if it is a necessary element of the loan process.

For example, a refinance transaction may require certain bills to be paid in full as part of the transaction. You will need to obtain the full account number for each account to confirm the pay off amount and to ensure that all payments are allocated correctly at the closing.

CREDIT HISTORY

E C O A	CREDITOR ACCOUNT NO	DATE RPTED	DATE LAST ACT	DATE OPND	LIMIT / HIGHEST CREDIT	PRESENT STATUS		·					
						BALANCE OWING	AMOUNT PAST DUE						
8	AFM-BLOOM #APRINTLO COLLEC-TION	02/99	04/94		425	425							

The date reported is the last reporting date for a particular account.

Not all creditors report on a monthly basis.

You may be required to bring the data pertaining to a specific account up to date to comply with specific underwriting requirements and to ensure that no derogatory data exists for the last months of the account.

The date last active provides you with information relating to the last date the account was in use.

Some accounts will be closed and will not effect of the transaction.

You should review the last active date before including the account in your history score.

The opening date of the account allows you to review the historical status with more accuracy.

The date opened may also help you to define when the homeowner began to have financial issues. This information is helpful when proving that the loss mitigation need is a result of a specific financial hardship and not an indication of poor planning or credit use on the part of the homeowner.

The present status details the current balances and any amounts currently due or past due for each account.

You should scan this column to note any issues that may arise during qualification and workout processes.

Past due accounts may lead to a lien against the subject property and should be considered during the workout planning.

The terms field shows you the original and the current agreement relating to the payments and terms of the account.

A revolving account or credit card will typically not provide you with an end date for the payments as these amounts will fluctuate depending on the borrower's spending actions.

If the account is an installment note, the column will give you the payment terms agreed upon for the account.

Payment amount will provide you with the minimum payment that is due on the account.

You will export these payment amounts into the debt-to-income ratio calculation form.

If the account has no payment entered, it may be an inactive account or it may be a revolving account that does not currently have a balance.

Even if an account does not have a balance, if credit is available to the borrower you must factor a minimum payment into the debt ratio for that account.

The underwriting guidelines will define the payment amount you will use.

E C O A	CREDITOR ACCOUNT NO	DATE RPTED	DATE LAST ACT	DATE OPND	LIMIT / HIGHEST CREDIT	PRESENT STATUS		TERMS	PAY AMT	TYPE AND ACCT STATUS	HISTORICAL STATUS			
						BALANCE OWING	AMOUNT PAST DUE				NO MOS HIIST REV	3 0	6 0	9 0
8	AFM-BLOOM #APRINTLO COLLEC-TION	02/99	04/94		425	425				OPN05				

HISTORICAL STATUS details allow you to review the credit history as well as determine if a specific credit issues exists in relationship to a particular account.

NO MOS HIST REV indicates the number of months detailed within the historical data section.

The numerical entries indicate the status of the payments to be found within the report.

Each account history will contain numbers indicating the status of a particular month's payment.

1 = on time
2 = 30 days late
3 = 60 days late
X = same as previous month

Read the history from LEFT to RIGHT.

Type and account status will provide you with the type of account and its present status.

- Revolving   REV
- Installment   Ins
- Mortgage   Mtg
- Consumer   Cons

This field could also contain derogatory accounts such as collections, charge offs or judgments.

- The number of month's history shows the numbers of months reported on the history of the account.

  Underwriting guidelines will dictate the number of months that must be reviewed for each account.

- When you review the account, you will be seeking the status of the account.

  In other words, you will review the account to determine whether the payments were made on time or if any late payment exists within the history.

- You will also look for the date of each payment reference.

  Minimal account history requirements may also exist.

  This column will enable you to determine if the borrower can meet these minimum credit requirements of the loan program you are considering.

- The historical status and late payments section provides you with numerical entries that indicate any late payments that will be found within the report.

  Each account history will contain numbers indicating the status of a particular month's payment.

  1 = on time

  2 = 30 days late

  3 = 60 days late

  X = the same status as the previous month

  This section of the history summary will provide you with the number of times a borrower has been on time, 30 days, and 60 days late during the reported credit history.

An account shows a 1 indicates that the account was paid on time within the history.

> ➤ When you note an account that contains derogatory information or a credit blemish, you should first confirm that the account is active and that the derogatory account is recent and the entry applies to the process.

> ➤ You will then determine the last date that the account is reported and begin counting backwards from the last entry.

You will review account details by moving from left to right.

Example: The reporting of this account begins in July.

The first entry is July. Moving backwards from Left to Right the next entries are

June	=	On Time
May	=	30 Days Late
April	=	On Time

and then backwards through time all of the payments were made on time.

Example: The next account was reported in June so the backwards counting will begin with the month of June.

You will need to obtain an update for this account that illustrates the payment in July to bring this account current with the other entries on the report.

When you locate an account that illustrates a late payment, you will enter a 1x30 day late into the status section of your credit history-scoring key.

You will complete this process for every account in the report that contains a derogatory entry. You will export any credit blemish or derogatory entry you find on the credit report into your credit history.

Many people find it helpful to note any derogatory or important data directly on the report prior to exporting this information onto the credit history-scoring key. This helps to ensure that you do not skip any important factors during the export processes.

Increasing the Score

Over time, a borrower can improve the information in his or her credit report

- by paying credit obligations as agreed and using credit wisely

- through the process of seasoning

  As derogatory data in the credit report gets older, it affects the score less

  A missed payment from four years ago will not count as much as a missed payment from six months ago.

- by using credit in a more controlled manner

  keeping debt load well below their maximum credit limits, their score is also likely to increase

A credit score, like a credit report, is a snapshot of an individual's changing credit record. If you make a request for a second repository report to get an updated score, the score is likely to change for many reasons. It is not possible to control how that score will change.

The credit items on the report are updated often, so new items are likely to have been added since the previous report.

Repeatedly requesting a borrower's credit report may substantially increase the number of inquiries on the repository report, which may affect the score adversely.

Removing Erroneous Information

Consumers who want to address what they believe is erroneous information on a credit report should contact the credit reporting agency which developed the report.

The Fair Credit Reporting Act (FCRA) allows the credit-reporting agency a "reasonable period of time", generally not to exceed 30 days, to investigate consumer disputed items.

A significant number of credit grantors use an automated system for investigating the disputes and respond to the dispute within a few days. Most credit reporting agencies make a special effort to resolve disputed information affecting a mortgage decision. The lender can weigh these factors and documentation provided by the borrower.

Because the score uses all the credit-related data on the credit bureau report and takes into account all contributing factors, removing or changing one specific, derogatory item will not guarantee an increase in Credit Bureau Score. In some cases, a change in the credit bureau report will have little or no effect on the score. Because there are many scorecards using a complex mathematical formula at each of the repositories, it is not possible to estimate how much the score will change if specific derogatory information is removed for a single repository report.

The number of inquiries may or may not be a factor in the score. When inquiries are a factor, they are typically not a strong one.

The law requires a record of all inquiries into the file be kept on file. This means inquiries cannot be removed from the credit report. Consumer disclosure inquiries are not used in determining score. It is up to the lender, as in all circumstances, to decide what a sufficient credit risk is.

COMPENSATING CONSIDERATIONS

When the potential buyer's situation does not meet the expectations, the seller has determined as the most desirable, some other factors may aid the seller in making a sound decision on the viability of the buyer.

The seller may choose to hold the mortgage by considering other factors in the buyer's profile. In conventional lending these additional pieces of information are commonly referred to as compensating factors.

It is up to the buyers to make as strong a case as possible for themselves based on any piece of information that will reflect favorably from the perspective of the seller. The following listing includes some items that could be considered compensating factors from the perspective of the seller. Remember that creative finance is just that, creative and that any item that positively reflects on the situation of the buyer has the potential to be considered a compensating factor by the seller.

Less than 10% increase for old rent/housing payments to the new housing expense

A decrease from the old rent/housing payments to the new housing expense

The borrower's excellent savings ability (as shown by savings accounts, etc)

3 or more months cash reserves

Larger than requested down payment

Residual income (excess after expense) of $500 per adult and $250 per child

Time at current residence exceeds 5 years

Time at current employment exceeds 5 years

Overall debt-to-income ratios are lower than the seller requires

Credit issues can be explained and documented because of an isolated incidence that is unlikely to recur

A perfect mortgage or rental history proven through the credit bureau

These are only examples of the most commonly used factors. Each situation has a different set of circumstances and it is up to the buyer and seller to determine what can be utilized to create the best possible contract for all parties involved.

DEBT-TO-INCOME RATIO'S

The debt ratio is what will determine "how much" loan a particular buyer can afford. The debt ratio is determined by comparing the current amount of money the buyer owes with the buyer's income to determine how much money is left to spend on a monthly basis.

Following are the two types of debt ratios that are often considered:

Front-End Ratio - this is the gross income divided by the new PITI mortgage payment.

In the conventional mortgage marketplace, the standard guideline is 29%.

For non-conforming (sub-prime) loan programs, the back-end debt ratio is more often used. This can be as high as 55% depending on the loan product being considered.

Back-End Ratio - this is the gross income divided by the new PITI mortgage payment and the minimum monthly payments from the other liabilities.

The standard guideline is 41% and the non-conforming guideline can be as high as 55% in the conventional mortgage marketplace.

It is important to remember that a higher debt ratio is another common reason a buyer will seek creative finance solutions.

Sellers may wish to review the debt-to-income ratio of the perspective buyer to determine if the potential risk is manageable. This is another important negotiating factor for both parties.

Following are the typical debts used to determine the qualifying ratios:

Front-End Ratios

The current and or future house payment

Back-End Ratios

The minimum required monthly payments on all of the following:

Auto Loans

Student Loans

Personal Loans

Charge Cards

Child Support

Alimony

Federal Tax Lien Repayment Schedules

Following are monthly liabilities that are not used to calculate debt ratios:

Utility Bills

Car & Health Insurance

Cell Phone Bills

The percentage of debts to income is called the debt-to-income (a.k.a. back-end) ratio.

An example of the income to debt calculation is as follows:

Income = $3,000

New Mortgage Payment = $900.

Minimum Monthly Payments = $300

"Mortgage" / "Income" = 30%

"Mortgage + Monthly Payments" / "Income" = 40%

In this scenario, your front-end is 30% and back-end is 40%, which is acceptable for many loan programs and can be considered acceptable to most sellers.

All the factors should be taken into account before any final decision concerning the offer is made. At times, the seller may determine a higher down payment or a higher monthly interest rate can offset the risk inherent in a high debt-to-income scenario.

Always keep in mind that the higher the interest rates the higher the monthly payment. In situations where the buyers overall monthly debt is at a level that is currently considered excessive, adding interest which will in turn inflate that monthly debt load may not be the wisest negotiating tactic.

DEBT TO INCOME RATIO (DTI%)

Monthly Income

Borrower		Co-Borrower	
$_____	Base Pay/ _____	$_____	Base Pay/ _____
$_____	Commission/_____	$_____	Commission/_____
$_____	Other _____	$_____	Other _____
$_____	Other _____	$_____	Other _____
$_____	Total Monthly Income	$_____	Total Monthly Income

Combined Monthly Income $_____

Monthly Debt

Borrower		Co-Borrower	
$_____	House/Rent Payment	$_____	House/Rent Payment
$_____	Automobile Payment	$_____	Automobile Payment
$_____	Credit Card _____	$_____	Credit Card _____
$_____	Credit Card _____	$_____	Credit Card _____
$_____	Credit Card _____	$_____	Credit Card _____
$_____	Personal Loan _____	$_____	Personal Loan _____
$_____	Other_____	$_____	Other_____
$_____	Other_____	$_____	Other_____
$_____	Total Monthly Debt	$_____	Total Monthly Debt

Combined Monthly Debt $_____

Take combined debt $_____ (factor each debt only once – if it is a joint debt list under the primary income earner only) and divide by the combined income $_____. The percentage _____% is your monthly debt-to-income ratio.

8:2 Sample Form DTI Ratio Assessment
This form is included for example purposes only. The services of a real estate professional should be retained to ensure the correct forms are used for your transaction.

CREDIT REPORT AUTHORIZATION AND RELEASE

Authorization is hereby granted to _____ to obtain a standard factual data credit report through a credit-reporting agency chosen by the
_____.

My signature below authorizes the release to the credit-reporting agency a copy of my credit application, and authorizes the credit-reporting agency to obtain information regarding my employment, savings accounts, and outstanding credit accounts (mortgages, auto loans, personal loans, charge cards, credit unions, etc.) Authorization is further granted to the reporting agency to use a Photostatted reproduction of this authorization if necessary to obtain any information regarding the above-mentioned information.

Applicants hereby request a copy of the credit report with any possible derogatory information be sent to the address of present residence, and holds
_____ and any credit reporting organization harmless in so mailing the copy requested.

Any reproduction of this credit authorization and release made by reliable means (for example photocopy or facsimile is considered an original.

_____   _____
Borrower's Signature   Borrower's Signature
Date: Date:
SSN: SSN:

_____   _____
Borrower's Signature   Borrower's Signature
Date: Date:
SSN: SSN:

8:3 Credit Report Authorization and Release
is form is included for example purposes only. The form is modified from the acceptable real estate forms as released by HUD. The services of a real estate professional should be retained to ensure the correct forms are used for your transaction.

Settlement and Costs

The settlement statement is the statement that itemizes all closing costs payable at the closing or settlement meeting.

The borrower and seller portions of the settlement statement will break down all expenses and receipts on each party's behalf.

The settlement statements should mirror the terms agreed upon during the contract negotiations.

Included in the seller's portion will be any liens or mortgages that must be paid to secure a clear title to the property, any seller concession toward the buyer's closing costs (as negotiated in the Sales Agreement) and any additional charges for which the seller is responsible.

The settlement statement contains the final figures pertaining to the transaction.

A reliable settlement company or real estate attorney typically prepares the settlement statement.

The settlement or closing company that prepares the final settlement statement should provide you with the figures on this final settlement statement 24 hours before your deal is set to close.

REAL ESTATE INVESTING – SELLER FINANCE

F. Type of Loan				
1__ FHA 2 __ FmHA 3__ Conv 4__ VA 5 __ Conv Ins	6. File Number:		7. Loan Number:	8. Mortgage Insurance Case Number

G.Note: This form is furnished to give you a statement of actual settlement costs. Amounts paid to and by the settlement agent are shown. Items marked "(P&C)" were paid outside the closing; they are shown here for informational purposes and are not included in the totals.

D. Name & Address of Borrower.	E. Name & Address of Seller	F. Name & Address of Lender
G. Property Location	H. Settlement Agent	I. Settlement Date
	Place of Settlement:	

J. Summary of Borrower's Transaction		**K. Summary of Seller's Transaction**	
100. Gross Amount Due From Borrower		**400. Gross Amount Due To Seller**	
101. Contract Sales Price		401. Contact Sales Price	
102. Personal Property		402. Personal Property	
103. Settlement Charges to borrower (line 1400)		403.	
104.		404.	
105.		405.	
Adjustments for items paid by seller in advance		Adjustments for items paid by seller in advance	
106. City / Town Taxes for		406. City / Town Taxes for	
107. County Taxes for		407. County Taxes for	
108. Assessments for		408. Assessments for	
109.		409.	
110.		410.	
111.		411.	
112.		412.	
120. Gross Amount Due From Borrower		**420. Gross Amount Due To Seller**	
200. Amounts Paid By Or In Behalf Of Borrower		**500. Reductions In Amount Due To Seller**	
201. Deposit or earnest money		501. Excess deposit (see instructions)	
202. Principal amount of new loan(s)		502. Settlement charges to seller (line 1400)	
203. Existing loan(s) take subject to		503. Existing loan(s) taken subject to	
204.		504. Payoff of first mortgage loan	
205.		505. Pay off of second mortgage loan	
206.		506.	
207.		507.	
208.		508.	
209.		509.	
Adjustments for items unpaid by seller		Adjustments for items unpaid by seller	
210. City / Town Taxes for		510. City / Town Taxes for	
211. County Taxes for		511. County Taxes for	
212. Assessments for		512. Assessments for	
213.		513.	
214.		514.	
215.		515.	
216.		516.	
217.		517.	
218.		518.	
219.		519.	
220. Total Paid By/For Borrower		**520. Total Reduction Amount Due Seller**	
300. Cash At Settlement From/To Borrower		**600. Cash at Settlement To/From Seller**	
301. Gross amount due from borrower (line 120)		601. Gross amount due to seller (line 420)	
302. Less amounts paid by/for borrower (line 220)	( )	602. Less reductions in amt due seller (line 520)	( )

9:1 Sample Form HUD-1 Settlement Statement
This form is included for example purposes only. The form is modified from the acceptable real estate forms as released by HUD. The services of a real estate professional should be retained to ensure the correct forms are used for your transaction.

	Paid From Borrowers Funds at Settlement	Paid From Seller's Funds at Settlement
700. Total Sales/Brokers commission based on price $ @ %		
Division of Commission (line 700) as follows:		
701. $ to		
702. $ to		
703 Commission paid at Settlement		
704.		
800. Items Payable in Connection with Loan		
801. Loan Origination Fee %		
802. Loan Discount %		
803. Appraisal Fee to		
804. Credit Report to		
805. Lender's Inspection Fee		
806. Mortgage Insurance Application Fee to		
807. Assumption Fee		
808.		
809.		
900. Items Required By Lender To Be Paid In Advance		
901. Interest from to @$ / day		
902. Mortgage Insurance Premium for months to		
903. Hazard Insurance Premium for years to		
904.		
905.		
1000. Reserves Deposited With Lender		
1001. Hazard Insurance months @$ per month		
1002. Mortgage Insurance months @$ per month		
1003. City Property Taxes months @$ per month		
1004. County Property Taxes months @$ per month		
1005. Annual Assessments months @$ per month		
1006. months @$ per month		
1007. months @$ per month		
1008. months @$ per month		
1100. Title Charges		
1101. Settlement or closing fee to		
1102. Abstract or title search to		
1103. Title examination to		
1104. Title insurance binder to		
1105. Document preparation to		
1106. Notary fees to		
1107. Attorney's fees to		
(includes above items numbers:)		
1108. Title Insurance to		
(includes above items numbers:)		
1109. Lender's coverage $		
1110. Owner's coverage $		
1111.		
1200. Government Recording and Transfer Charges		
1201. Recording fees: Deed $: Mortgage $: Releases $		
1202. City/county tax/stamps: Deed $: Mortgage $		
1203. State tax/stamps: Deed $: Mortgage $		
1204.		
1205.		
1300. Additional Settlement Charges		
1301. Survey to		
1302. Pest Inspection to		
1303.		
1304.		
1400. Total Settlement Charges (enter on lines 103, Section J and 502, Section K)		

9:2 Sample Form –

HUD -1 Settlement Statement Page 2 This form is included for example purposes only. The form is modified from the acceptable real estate forms as released by HUD. The services of a real estate professional should be retained to ensure the correct forms are used for your transaction.

Page one section 100 will contain the total of all costs involved with the loan process. These will include the sales price, settlement charges, and any pro-rated taxes due or owed.

The seller's portion of the settlement statement breaks down all items on the seller's behalf. Included in the seller's portion will be:

- Any liens or mortgages that must be paid to secure a clear title to the property

- any seller concession toward the buyer's closing costs (as negotiated in the Sales Agreement) and any additional charges for which the seller is responsible.

- Any prorated items the seller has agreed to pay as negotiated in the sales agreement.

- Any other costs the seller has incurred that must be paid at the closing table.

Page two of the settlement statement contains a more detailed breakdown of the charges included in the section titled settlement charges to borrower and seller.

The fees and costs being charges in relationship to the transaction will be included in this section.

Upon confirming that the settlement statement is in agreement with the terms negotiated on the sales agreement, the buyer and seller should notify the settlement agent that the statement is approved and the closing can go forward.

The buyer will need to obtain a certified check in the amount due form borrower to bring to the closing or settlement.

All parties will need to bring a valid ID that contains a photograph to verify the identity of each party to the person notarizing all documents.

Following is a detailed explanation of the format and items included in the settlement statement.

Page one section 100 will contain the total of all costs involved with the loan process.

These will include:

- The sales price

- Settlement charges

- Any pro-rated taxes due from the borrower

Section 200 will contain all amounts, which are paid on behalf of the borrower. These will include:

- Any deposit or earnest money the borrower paid at the time of the Sales Agreement negotiation.

- Any additional deposits or payments made by the borrower in the course of the negotiation meeting.

- The loan amount as negotiated with the seller and to be finalized with a note as part of the settlement meeting.

- Any assumed loans the borrower is taking.

- Any closing costs to be paid by the seller as negotiated at the time of the Sales Agreement.

- Any additional adjustments that the Title Company has determined must be made to the finances of the package.

The figures will be calculated, taking the amount paid on behalf of the borrower (#220) and the amount due from the borrower (120) to determine the exact figure the borrower is required to bring to the closing table.

Page two of the settlement statement contains a more detailed breakdown of the charges included in the section titled settlement charges to borrower. The fees and costs being charges on the loan will be included in this section. These figures will mirror the figures created during the negotiation process making an error relatively simple to find.

L.   SETTLEMENT CHARGES

700.   TOTAL SALES/BROKER'S COMMISSION based on price $ @ %= PAID FROM BORROWER'S FUNDS AT SETTLEMENT PAID FROM SELLER'S FUNDS AT SETTLEMENT

701.   Division of the commission   These commission figures will typically be paid to the real estate agent.

                                        This charge will appear only if an agent was used in the negotiation process.

702.   Division of the commission

703.   Commission paid at Settlement

704.

800.   Items Payable in Connection
        with Loan: These are the fees that lenders
                                            charge to process, approve and make the mortgage loan

801.   Loan Origination   This fee is usually known as a loan origination fee
                                            but sometimes is called a "point" or "points."

                                            It is paid to the lender if a lender exists in the transaction.

802.   Loan Discount   Also often called "points" or "discount points," a
                                            loan discount is a one-time charge imposed by the lender or
                                            broker to lower the rate at which the lender or broker would
                                            otherwise offer the loan.

                                            This charge appears only if a lender exists in the transaction.

803.   Appraisal Fee   This charge pays for an appraisal report made by an
                                            appraiser.

805.   Credit Report Fee   This fee covers the cost of a credit report.

806.   Lender's Inspection Fee   This charge covers inspections, often of newly
                                            constructed housing, made by employees of the lender or by
                                            an outside inspector.

                                            Pest or other inspections made by companies other than the
                                            lender are discussed in line 1302.

807.   Mortgage Insurance
        Application Fee   This fee covers the processing of an application for mortgage
                                            insurance.

808.   Assumption Fee   This is a fee, which is charged when a buyer
                                            "assumes" or takes over the duty to pay the seller's existing
                                            mortgage loan.

809.   Mortgage Broker Fee   Fees paid to mortgage brokers would be listed here.

900.   Items Required by Lender to Be Paid in Advance:

Certain items may require payment at the time of settlement, such as accrued interest, mortgage insurance premiums, and hazard insurance premiums.

901.   Interest   The interest that accrues from the date of settlement
                                         to the first monthly payment.

902.   Mortgage Insurance
       Premium   The first years mortgage insurance premium or a lump sum
                                         up-front premium.

903.   Hazard Insurance Premium   Hazard insurance protects against loss due to fire,
                                         windstorm, and natural hazards.

904.   Flood Insurance   If the property requires flood insurance, the
                                         premium is usually listed here.

1000   RESERVES DEPOSITED WITH LENDER:

These lines identify the payment of taxes and/or insurance and other items that must be made at settlement to set up an escrow account.

1001   Hazard Insurance   months @ $ per month

1002. Mortgage insurance   months @ $ per month

1003. City property taxes   months @ $ per month

1004. County property taxes   months @ $ per month

1005. Annual assessments   months @ $ per month

1006.   months @ $ per month

1007.   months @ $ per month

1008. Aggregate Adjustment

1100. Title Charges: Title charges may cover a variety of services
                                     performed by title companies and others.

1101. Settlement or Closing Fee   This fee is paid to the settlement agent or escrow
                                     holder.

Responsibility for payment of this fee should be negotiated between the seller and the buyer.

1102-
1104. Abstract of Title/
Title Examination/
Title Binder   The charges on these lines cover the costs of the title search and examination.

1105. Document Preparation   This is a separate charged to cover the costs of preparation of final legal papers, such as a mortgage, deed of trust, note or deed.

1106. Notary Fee   This fee is charged for the cost of having a person who is licensed as a notary public swears to the fact that the persons named in the documents did, in fact, sign them.

1107. Attorney's Fees   The cost of any attorney appears here.

1108. Title Insurance   The total cost of owner's and lender's title insurance is shown here.

1109. Lender's Title Insurance The cost of the lender's policy is shown here.

1105. Owner's (Buyer's)
Title Insurance: The cost of the new owner's policy is shown here.

1200. Government Recording and Transfer Charges:

Transfer taxes, which in some localities are collected whenever property changes hands or a mortgage loan is made, are set by state and/or local governments. City, county and/or state tax stamps may have to be purchased as well (lines 1202 and 1203).

1201. Recording fees   Deed $; Mortgage $; Releases $

1202. City/county tax/stamps Deed $; Mortgage $

1203. State tax/stamps   Deed $; Mortgage $

1204.

1205.

1301. Additional Settlement Charges:

1302. Survey

If it is required that a surveyor conduct a property survey the cost is entered here.

1303. Pest and Other Inspections

This fee is to cover inspections for termites or other pest infestation.

1304. Lead-Based Paint Inspections

This fee is to cover inspections or evaluations for lead-based paint hazard risk assessments and may be on any blank line in the 1300 series.

1400. Total Settlement Charges:

The sum of all fees in the borrower's column entitled "Paid from Borrower's Funds at Settlement" is placed here.

This figure is then transferred to line 103 of Section J, "Settlement charges to borrower" in the Summary of Borrower's Transaction on page 1 of the HUD-1 Settlement Statement and added to the purchase price.

The sum of all of the settlement fees paid by the seller are transferred to line 502 of Section K, Summary of Seller's Transaction on page 1 of the HUD-1 Settlement Statement.

Paid Outside Of Closing ("POC"): Some fees may be listed on the HUD-1 to the left of the borrower's column and marked "P.O.C." Fees such as those for credit reports and appraisals are usually paid by the borrower before closing/settlement.

The first page of the HUD-1 Settlement Statement summarizes all the costs and adjustments for the borrower and seller.

Section J   is the summary of the borrower's transaction.

Section K   is the summary of the seller's side of the transaction.

Section 100   summarizes the borrower's costs, such as

the contract cost of the house

any personal property being purchased

the total settlement charges owed by the borrower from Section L.

Line 106   adjustments are made for items such as

        Taxes

        Assessments

        Fuel

that the seller has previously paid and for which the borrower will reimburse the seller.

10
CHAPTER

Deeds

As we explained earlier in the course, the handling of the deed during a seller finance transaction is open for negotiations. Regardless of the method of deed transfer, you agree upon, you must understand more fully, what a deed means in a real estate transaction.

There are a various deeds that can be offered by the seller. Each type of deed carries different connotations, responsibilities, and warranties. Some examples of commonly used deeds are shown on the following pages.

GENERAL WARRANTY DEED: This is typically the best deed to obtain from the perspective of the buyer.

This deed states that the Grantor (seller) warrants good, clear title to the grantee (buyer) and agrees to protect the grantee from any defect in the title whether the defect occurred during the seller's ownership or that of previous owners.

SPECIAL WARRANTY DEED: The grantor warrants good, clear title to the grantee and agrees to protect and defend the grantee from all defects in the title that occurred during the grantor's ownership.

In other words, the seller is guaranteeing that he has cleared the title from all defects during his ownership but is making no guarantees as to the condition of the title because of the actions of previous owners.

BARGAIN AND SALE DEED: The grantor implies that he owns an interest in the property but conveys the property without any warranty to the grantee.

In this case, it would be most prudent to have a professional title search performed.

These deeds are often used for quick transfer and carry no guarantees as to the condition of the title.

QUITCLAIM DEED: This type of deed is used when the transaction is completed quickly.

These can also be used to remove the interest of a party in a creative finance scenario.

Some buyers who default on the creative finance agreement may be willing to return any interest in the property to the seller in lieu of foreclosure by using a quitclaim deed.

In a quitclaim deed, the Grantor coveys whatever interests or claims they have in a property without any warranty or even the implication that they own a portion of the property.

These deeds are frequently used in an effort to clear title blemishes of perceived claims when a property is being transferred.

A deed will typically carry some key components, which aid in making it a legal document and protect both parties to the terms of the negotiations.

A deed must contain some components to qualify as a recordable document under the guidelines of many clerks of courts recording requirements. The following pages provide a sample of a deed and a breakdown of the components that must be included.

Private as well as public property transfer transactions can benefit from the use of a professional in the preparation of the deed document to ensure compliance with all of the regulations.

NAMES: The names of the parties, both the buyers and the sellers, must be included on the deed.

This section should be fully completed and concise.

Marital status and any name changes should be included in this portion of the deed.

Name changes can be noted as "formerly known as..."

CONSIDERATION: A statement that the property is being sold for payment must be included.

This is the purchase price of the property.

Some Jurisdictions allow you to may maintain the privacy of the transfer by inserting a nominal amount of money plus the statement "other consideration".

A phrase such as "$1.00 plus other good and valuable consideration" would be valid in jurisdictions that allow this type of privacy statement.

GRANTING CLAUSE: This states what act the parties are performing, in other words this clause signifies the intent of the seller to convey the property to the buyer

LEGAL DESCRIPTION: This is a very exact description of the property, not the physical address, which allows one to locate and identify the property to be conveyed and distinguishes the property from all other real estate.

RECITAL: This identifies previous owners from whom the current grantor took title.

It aids in obtaining a chain of title by reciting backwards from this transaction to allow a searcher to find the next piece in the chain in reverse.

REALTY TAX STAMPS: These are obtained at the courthouse of record and are essential to the recordation of the deed.

These provide proof that the state and local taxes to transfer real property have been paid.

TO HAVE AND TO HOLD CLAUSE: This is also know as the habendum and is the technical language that describes the ownership that is being transferred.

GRANTOR'S SIGNATURE: The grantors (sellers) are the parties who must sign the deed.

No signature of acceptance by the grantee (buyer) must be included to affect a legal transfer.

ACKNOWLEDGEMENT: This is best known as notarizing and is the event where the sellers appear before a notary or other approved person to prove and declare that the signing of the deed and the transfer of said deed is a voluntary act.

CERTIFICATE OF GRANTEE ADDRESS: This is another requirement, which must be fulfilled in order to record the deed.

This provides the new owner information, which allows the taxing authorities to send all future notices and tax bills to the grantee.

RECORDING REFERENCE: This is typically included by the clerk of record and specifies the

date

deed-book volume

deed-book page number

where the recorded document is filed.

DELIVERY AND ACCEPTANCE: While there is no requirement that the grantees sign the deed document, the last legal step in the transfer of the deed is the delivery and acceptance of the conveyance is that the grantee must receive and accept the document.

This acceptance finalizes the transaction and conveyance of the property has been achieved.

SAMPLE OF A BASIC WARRANTY DEED

For good consideration, we (I) _____ of
_____, County of _____, State of
_____, hereby bargain, deed and convey to _____ of
_____, County of _____, State of
_____, the following described land in _____ county,
free and clear with WARRANTY COVENANTS; to wit:

Grantor, for itself and its heirs, hereby covenants with Grantee, its heirs, and assigns, that Grantor is lawfully seized in fee simple of the above-described premises; that it has a good right to convey; that the premises are free from all encumbrances; that Grantor and its heirs, and all persons acquiring any interest in the property granted, through or for Grantor, will, on demand of Grantee, or its heirs or assigns, and at the expense of Grantee, its heirs or assigns, execute and instrument necessary for the further assurance of the title to the premises that may be reasonably required; and that Grantor and its heirs will forever warrant and defend all of the property so granted to Grantee, its heirs, against every person lawfully claiming the same or any part thereof.

Being the same property conveyed to the Grantors by deed of _____, dated
_____, 20____ .

WITNESS the hands and seal of said Grantors this _____ day of _____, 20____ .

_____
Grantor

_____
Grantee

STATE OF _____

COUNTY OF _____

On_____before me,_____, personally appeared
_____, personally known to me (or proved to me on the basis of satisfactory evidence) to be the person(s) whose name(s) is/are subscribed to the within instrument and acknowledged to me that he/she/they executed the same in his/her/their authorized capacity(ies), and that by his/her/their signature(s) on the instrument the person(s), or the entity upon behalf of which the person(s) acted, executed the instrument.

WITNESS my hand and official seal.

Signature_____
Affiant _____Known _____Unknown
ID Produced_____

10:1 Sample Form Basic Warranty Deed

This form is included for example purposes only. The form is modified from the acceptable real estate forms as released by HUD. The services of a real estate professional should be retained to ensure the correct forms are used for your transaction.

Before entering any transaction agreement, both parties should obtain a thorough understanding of the public records system and recording process. All states have recording acts, which govern processes of the recording of documents pertaining to the transfer of real estate. These documents are on file at the Recorder of Deeds office in the county courthouse that governs the region in which the property is located.

Some of the documents, which you may need to record during your transaction, include:

Mortgages	Notes	Long Term Leases
Options	Deeds	Land Contracts

Additional documents, which may occur in the transaction but are less common include:

Easements	Additional Liens	Plot Plans

When requesting the recordation of a document at the courthouse, you will pay recording fees. The amount of the recording fee will vary by region across the country. You should contact your county court offices to determine the actual costs for your area.

All documents are recorded in a chronological or time based order.

This allows for easier research of the chain of title.

Each document will have a date and time stamp as well as a book and page number.

The documents will be photocopied and the copies will be placed in the noted book with indexes created to aid in future location of the documents.

The original copy of the recorded instrument will be returned to the owner for their records.

Earlier we discussed deeds and the variety of warranties that a seller may include. Regardless of the warranty, a title examination is recommended. A through title examination allows the buyer to determine the true ownership of the property and ensure the sellers rights to sell the property. It also shows the quality of the title. In other words, it shows the condition of the title during the current ownership as well as under previous owners.

An individual can perform a title examination, but there are professional examiners who are trained to determine the key components that may affect the ownership transfer of a property. If you plan to perform the title examination yourself, it is recommended that you complete a course designed to teach title-abstracting basics. The process of searching a title is a very detailed and complicated undertaking and in many cases, it is recommended that a trained professional be involved in this process.

Regardless of who is completing the search, an abstract of title should be completed. We will cover the three basic components of an abstract of title that bear scrutiny:

Chain of Title	The chain of title should be traced.
	The chain of title is the linking together of all previous owners of a property.
	As stated earlier the grantee to the seller is typically included on each deed recorded. Therefore, the previous owners should be easily located to trace back from the current deed to the original granting of the land.
Defects	Any defects in the title should be noted.
	Each previous owner's term of ownership should be scrutinized to uncover any defects, which could include

> unpaid mortgages
>
> unpaid liens
>
> easements
>
> lawsuits
>
> other items that may effect or encumber the property being transferred.

Status of Defects	The last item that should be researched is the status of the defects.
	This means that, once a defect is found, the outcome of the defect should be researched. Mortgages, liens, lawsuits etc, may be settled or they may remain or have been changed but still exist.

This research allows both the buyer and the seller to understand the condition of the title to be transferred.

If the abstract is completed by a professional, title insurance will often be offered.

In case of a mortgage or financing through conventional lending sources, title insurance is often required for the protection of the lending institution.

Title insurance protects against any loss due to defects in the title that may become known in the future.

Lender required title insurance protects the interest of the lender.

Title insurance can be issued to protect the buyer as well.

In a private transaction, it may be wise to purchase title insurance to ensure the status of the buyer.

The decision to have the title researched by a professional or to obtain insurance on the title is a private decision that must be negotiated at the time of the sale of the property.

GLOSSARY OF FINANCE TERMS

1-year ARM: An adjustable-rate mortgage (ARM) that has an initial interest rate for one year, and thereafter has an adjustment interval of one year. The adjustment is based on comparison interest caps and the indexed rate

3/1 ARM: An adjustable-rate mortgage (ARM) that has an initial interest rate for three years, and thereafter has an adjustment interval of one year. The adjustment is based on comparison interest caps and the indexed rate.

5/1 ARM: An adjustable-rate mortgage (ARM) that has an initial interest rate for five years, and thereafter has an adjustment interval of one year. The adjustment is based on comparison interest caps and the indexed rate

7/1 ARM: An adjustable-rate mortgage (ARM) that has an initial interest rate for seven years, and thereafter has an adjustment interval of one year. The adjustment is based on comparison interest caps and the indexed rate

10/1 ARM: An adjustable-rate mortgage (ARM) that has an initial interest rate for ten years, and thereafter has an adjustment interval of one year. The adjustment is based on comparison interest caps and the indexed rate

Abstract of Title: A written history of all the transactions that bear on the title to a specific piece of land An abstract of title covers the time from when the property was first sold to the present. Used by the Title Company to produce a title binder

Acceleration Clause: The section of a mortgage document that allows the lender to speed up the payment date in the event of default, making the entire principal amount due

Acre: An area of land 43.560 square feet

Adjustable Rate Mortgage: Mortgage in which the rate of interest is adjusted based on a standard rate index. Most ARM's have caps on how much the interest rate may increase

Adjustment Interval: How often the loan's rate can be changed

Alternative Mortgage: 7/23 and 5/25 mortgages with a one-time rate adjustment after seven years and five years respectively Also known as a hybrid mortgage or a two-step mortgage

Amortization Schedule : A timetable for the gradual repayment of a mortgage loan An amortization schedule indicates the amount of each payment applied to interest and principal, and the remaining balance after each payment is made

Amortization Term: The amount of time required to amortize (repay) a mortgage loan. The amortization term is usually expressed in months. A 30-year fixed rate mortgage, for example, has an amortization term of 360 months

Annual Percentage Rate (APR): A standardized method of calculating the cost of a mortgage, stated as a yearly rate which includes such items as interest, mortgage insurance, and certain points or credit costs

Appraisal: A written report by a qualified appraiser estimating the value of the property

Appraised Value: An opinion of a property's fair market value, based on an appraiser's inspection and analysis of the property

Appraiser: A person qualified by education, training, and experience to estimate the value of real property

Appreciation: An increase in the value of a property due to changes in market conditions or improvements to the property

ARM: See Adjustable Rate Mortgage

Assessed Value: The value of a property as determined by a public tax assessor for the purpose of taxation

Assumable: A mortgage that a buyer can assume, or take over, from the seller of the property

Balloon Mortgage: A loan that has regular monthly payments, which amortize over a stated term but call for a final lump sum (balloon payment) at the end of a specified term, or maturity date such as 10 years

Basis Points: 1/100th of 1 percent If an interest rate changes 50 basis points, for example, it has move ½ of 1 percent

Binder: See title binder

Biweekly Mortgage: A mortgage that schedules payments every two weeks instead of the standard monthly payment The 26 biweekly payments are each equal to one-half of the monthly payment. The result for the borrower is a substantial reduction in interest payments because the mortgage is paid off sooner. See also prepayment plan

Bridge loan: A loan that "bridges" the gap between the purchase of a new home and the sale of the borrower's current home. The borrower's current home is used as collateral and the money is used to close on the new home before the current home is sold. Some are structured so they completely pay off the old home's first mortgage at the bridge loan's closing. Others pile the new debt on top of the old. They usually run for a term of six months

Broker: See mortgage broker

Broker Premium: A premium paid to the mortgage broker as the "middleman" in the mortgage process between the lender and the borrower

Built-ins: Cabinets, ranges, ceiling fans and other items permanently attached to the structure, and which a buyer may assume will remain with the structure

Buy down: The process of trading money for a lower mortgage rate The borrower "buys down" the interest rate on a mortgage by paying discount points up front. It can also be a mortgage in which an initial lump sum payment is made to reduce a borrower's monthly payments during the first few years of a mortgage

Caps: The maximum amount the interest rate can change annually or cumulatively over the life of an adjustable rate mortgage. F or example, if the caps are 2 percent annual and 6 percent life of loan, a mortgage with a first-year rate of 10 percent could rise to no more than 12 percent the second year, and no more than 16 percent over the entire life of the loan

Certificate of Title: A statement provided by the Title Company or attorney stating that the title to the real estate is legally held by the current owner

Chattel: Personal property

Clear title: A title that is free of liens or legal questions as to ownership of a piece of property

Closing: The meeting at which the sale of a property is finalized The buyer signs the lender agreement for the mortgage and pays' closing costs and escrow amounts. The buyer and seller sign documents to transfer the ownership of the property. Also known as the settlement

Closing costs: Expenses incurred by buyers and sellers in transferring ownership of a property. Closing costs normally include an origination fee, an attorney's fee, taxes, escrow payments, and charges for title insurance. Lenders or Real Estate Agents provide estimates of closing costs to prospective homebuyers

Closing Statement: A financial disclosure accounting for all funds changing hands at the closing See also HUD-1 Statement

Cloud on title: Any fact or condition that could adversely affect the title

Commission: In real estate, the broker, or mortgage associates fee for assisting in the transaction Usually expressed as a percentage of the total paid by the buyer

Commitment: A formal offer by a lender stating the approved terms for lending money to a homebuyer

Common Area Assessment: A levy against individual unit owners in a condominium or planned unit development to pay for upkeep, repairs, and improvements to the property's common areas, such as corridors, elevators, parking lots, swimming pools and tennis courts

Comparables: Refers to "comparable properties" which are used for comparative purposes in the appraisal process. Comps are recently sold properties that are similar in size, location, and amenities to the home for sale. Comps help an appraiser determine the fair market value of a property

Condominium: A real estate project in which each unit owner has title to a unit of the project, and sometimes and undivided interest in the common areas

Conforming Loan: A loan that conforms to the standard rules for purchase by Freddie Mac or Fannie Mae

Contingency: A condition that must be met before a contract is legally binding. For example, homebuyers often include a contingency that specifies that the contract is not binding until after a satisfactory report from a home inspector

Contract: In real estate parlance, the contract is the legal document by which buyer and seller make offers and counteroffers. The real estate contract describes the property, includes or excludes items in the property, names the price, apportions the closing costs between the parties and sets forth a closing date. When a buyer and seller agree on the terms and sign the same document the property is said to be "under contract". More formally known as the agreement for the sale, purchase agreement, or earnest money contract

Conventional Mortgage: Usually refers to a fixed-rate, 30-year mortgage that is not insured by FHA, Farmers Home Administration, or Veterans Administration

Convertible Mortgage: An adjustable rate mortgage ARM that can be converted to a fixed mortgage under specific conditions

Cooperative: A type of multiple ownership in which the residents of a multiunit housing complex own shares in the cooperative corporation that owns the property, giving each resident the right to occupy a specific apartment or unit

Cost-of-funds: A yield index based upon the cost of funds to savings & loan institution in the San Francisco Federal Home Loan Bank District. It is one of the indexes commonly used to set the rate of adjustable rate mortgages

Covenant: A written restriction on the use of land, most commonly in use today in homeowners associations

Credit report: A report on a person's credit history prepared by a credit bureau and used by a lender in determining a loan applicant's record for paying debts in a timely manner

Debt-to-Income Ratio: The percentage of a person's monthly earnings used to pay off all debt obligations Lenders consider two ratios, constructed in slightly different ways. The first called the front-end ratio, the ratio of the monthly housing expenses – including principal, interest, property taxes, and insurance, (PITI) is compared to the borrower's gross, pretax monthly income. In the back-end ratio, a borrower's other debts such as auto loans and credit cards are figured in. Lenders usually consider both and set an acceptable ratio. Some lenders and some lending qualifying agencies only consider the back-end ratio

Deed: The legal document conveying title to the property

Depreciation: A decline in the value of a property as opposed to appreciation

Discount Points: A type of point (1 percent of the loan) paid by the borrower to reduce the interest rate

Down payment: The amount of a property's purchase price that the buyer pays in cash and does not finance with a mortgage

Earnest money: A deposit made by potential homebuyers during negotiations with the seller. The sum shows a seller that the buyer is serious about purchasing a property

Easement: The right of another to use a property The most common easements are for utility lines

80-10-10 Loan: A combination of an 80 percent loan-to-value first mortgage, a 10 percent down payment and a 10 percent home equity loan. This is also sometimes referred to as a CLTV (Combined Loan-to-Value)

Encumbrance: A lien, charge, or liability against a property

Equal Credit: A federal law that requires lenders and other creditors to make credit equally available with out discrimination based on race, color, religion, national origin, age, sex, marital status, or receipt of income from public assistance programs

Equity: The value of a homeowner's unencumbered interest in real estate Equity is the difference between the homes fair market value and the unpaid balance of the mortgage and any outstanding liens

Equity increases as the mortgage is paid down or as the property enjoys appreciation

Escrow Payment: The portion of a homeowner's monthly mortgage payment that is held by the loan servicer to pay for taxes and insurance Also known as reserves The loan servicer holds the escrow funds separately from money meant to pay principal and interest

Fair Credit Reporting Act: A consumer protection law that regulates the disclosure of consumer credit reports by credit reporting agencies and establishes procedures for correcting mistakes on a person's credit record

Fannie Mae: Nickname for Federal National Mortgage Association It is a government-chartered non-bank financial services company and the nation's largest source of financing for home mortgages It was started to make sure mortgage money is available in all areas of the country

FHA Mortgage: A mortgage insured by the Federal Housing Administration

First mortgage: A mortgage that is the primary lien against a property

Fixed-rate Mortgage: A mortgage in which the interest rate does not change during the entire term of the loan, most often 15, or 30 years

Flood Insurance   Insurance that compensates for the physical property damage resulting from rising water It is required for properties located in federally designated flood areas

Foreclosure: The legal process by which a homeowner in default on a mortgage is deprived of interest in the property This usually involves a forced sale of the property at public auction with the proceeds of the sale being applied to the mortgage debt

Freddie Mac: Nickname for Federal Home Loan Mortgage Corp A financial corporation chartered by the federal government to buy pools of mortgages from lenders and sell securities backed by these mortgages

Ginnie Mae: Nickname for the Government National Mortgage Association

Good Faith Estimate: A written estimate of closing costs that the lender must provide to prospective homebuyers within three days of submitting a mortgage loan application

Government National Mortgage Association (Ginnie Mae) A government-owned corporation within the US Department of Housing and Urban Development (HUD) Created by Congress in 1968, GNMA has responsibility for the special assistance loan program known as Ginnie Mae

Hazard Insurance: Insurance coverage that compensates for physical damage to property from natural disasters such as fire and other hazards Depending on where a piece of property is located, lenders may also require flood insurance or policies covering windstorms (hurricanes) or earthquakes

Home Inspection: An inspection by a building professional that evaluates the structural and mechanical condition of a property

Homeowners Association: A nonprofit association that manages the common areas of a condominium or PUD Unit owners pay the association a fee to maintain areas owned jointly

Homeowner's Insurance: An insurance policy that combines personal liability insurance and hazard insurance coverage for a residence and its contents

Housing Expense: The percentage of gross monthly income that goes toward paying a Ratio mortgage or rent on a home

HUD-1: The document with an itemized listing of closing costs payable at the closing or settlement meeting when buying property The closing costs can include a commission, loan fees, and points, and sums set aside for escrow payments, taxes, and insurance It is signed by both the buyer and the seller, who may be paying some of the closing costs The statement form is published by HUD

Hybrid Mortgage: See alternative mortgage products.

Index: A published measure of the cost of money that lenders use to calculate the rate on an ARM The most common indexes are the one-year Treasury Constant Maturity Yield and the FHLB 11th District Cost of Funds

Indexed Rate: The sum of the published index plus the margin For example, if the index were 9 percent and the margin 2.75 percent, the indexed rate would be 11.75 percent. Often, lenders charge less than the indexed rate the first year of an ARM

Initial Interest Rate: Starting rate of an ARM

Interest Tax Deduction: Most mortgage holders can deduct all the interest paid on the loan in filing income tax The deduction applies to people with just on mortgage on a primary residence, as well as those with a combination of loans. Within certain time limits set by the IRS, points paid up front on a mortgage are usually deductible in the year the house was purchased

Jumbo Mortgage: Mortgages larger than the limits set by Fannie Mae and Freddie Mac. A jumbo mortgage will carry a higher interest rate than a conventional mortgage

Lease-purchase   A financing option that allows a potential homebuyer to lease a property with the option to buy   Often constructed so the monthly rent payment covers the owner's first mortgage payment, plus an additional amount as a savings deposit to accumulate cash for a down payment   A seller may agree to a lease-purchase option if the housing market is saturated and the seller is having a difficult time selling the property

Lien: A legal hold or claim from one person on the property of another The lien placed by a first mortgage is special. It is called a first lien and takes precedence over others

Lifetime Rate Cap: In an ARM, it limits the amount that the interest rate can increase or decrease over the life of the loan. See also caps

Lis Pendens: A pending lawsuit; in real estate, the constructive notice filed in public records that a legal dispute exists over a piece of property

Livery of Seizen: Under common law, the process of transferring title

Loan Origination: The process by which a mortgage lender obtains a mortgage secured by real property An origination fee is charged by the lender to process all forms involved in obtaining a mortgage

Loan-to-value (LTV) Ratio: The ratio of a mortgage loan amount to the property's appraised value or selling price, whichever is less For example, if a home is sold for $100,000 and the mortgage amount is $80,000 the LTV is 80%

Lock: Lender's guarantee that the mortgage rate quoted will be good for a specific amount of time. The homebuyer usually wants the lock to stay in effect until the date of the closing

Lock-and-Float: Rate programs offered by companies that allow borrowers to lock in the current interest rate on a mortgage for a specified period, while also letting them "float" the rate down if market conditions improve before closing

Low-down Mortgages: Mortgages with a low down payment, usually less than 10 percent. Frannie Mae and Freddie Mac design loan programs that spell out a set of standards for lenders. In recent years, these government-chartered agencies have made low-down mortgages more available

Margin: The number of percentage points added to the index on a one-year ARM

Maturity: The date on which the principal balance of a loan becomes due and payable

Mortgage: A legal document that uses property as collateral to secure payment of a debt

Mortgage Banker: The lender that originates a mortgage loan, the one making the loan directly, and closing the loan

Mortgage Broker: An individual or company that brings borrowers and lenders together for the purpose of loan origination Unlike a mortgage banker, brokers do not fund the loan but work on behalf of several lenders. Brokers typically require a fee or a commission for their service See broker premium

Mortgage Insurance: A policy that insures the lender against loss should the homeowner default on a mortgage. Depending on the loan, the insurance can be issued by government agencies such as the FHA or a private company. It is part of the monthly mortgage payment. (See also private mortgage insurance PMI)

Negative Amortization: A gradual increase in mortgage debt that happens when a monthly payment does not cover the entire principal and interest due The shortfall is added to the remaining balance to create "negative" amortization

No-doc or low-doc Loan: These no-documentation or low-documentation loans are designed for the entrepreneur or self-employed, for recent immigrants with money in foreign countries or for borrowers who cannot or choose not to reveal information about their incomes

Note: The document giving evidence of mortgage indebtedness, including the amount and terms of repayment

Origination Fee: A fee paid to the lender for processing a loan application

Owner financing A transaction in which the seller of a house provides all or part of the financing Sellers may provide financing because they need to sell the property right away or they are having difficulty selling the house and want to provide financing as an incentive to a buyer

Periodic rate cap: In an ARM, it limits how much an interest rate can increase or decrease during any one-adjustment period See also caps

PITI: Stands for principal, interest, taxes and insurance that are the usual components of a monthly mortgage payment

PITI Reserves: A cash amount that a homebuyer must have on hand after making a down payment and paying all closing costs. The reserves required by a lender must equal the amount a buyer would pay for PITI for a specific number of months

Plat: A map that shows a parcel of land and how it is subdivided into individual lots Plat maps also show the locations of streets and easements

PMI: See private mortgage insurance

Points: A point equals 1 percent of a mortgage loan. Lenders charge points as a way to make a profit. Borrowers may pay discount points to reduce the loan interest rate. Buyers are prohibited from paying points on HUD or VA guaranteed loans

Pre-approval: This process goes a step further than pre-qualification. It means the lender has contacted the borrower's employer, bank, and other places to verify all claims of earnings and assets. In return, the borrower receives a letter stating the lender is willing to grant a mortgage for a specific amount within a limited period with the stipulation that there are no material changes to the borrower's situation

Prepayment Penalty: A fee imposed by certain lenders if the first mortgage is paid off early

Prepayment Plan: Similar to biweekly mortgage, but operated by a third party In it, the borrower pays to the third party, half the monthly mortgage payment every two weeks At the end of the year, the plan operators typically take the extra money that results from the process and sends lump sum payment to the participants' lenders

Pre-qualification: An early evaluation by a lender of a potential homebuyer's credit report, plus earnings, savings, and debt information The homebuyer gets a non-binding estimate of the mortgage amount the borrower would qualify for, or how much house the borrower can afford. Buyers who pre-qualify can go a step further and seek a pre-approval

Rate Lock: A commitment issued by a lender to the homebuyer or the mortgage broker guaranteeing a specific interest rate for a specified amount of time See also lock

Real Estate Agent: A person licensed to negotiate and transact the sale of real estate on behalf of the property owner

RESPA: Real Estate Settlement Procedures Act A consumer protection law that requires lenders to give homebuyers advance notice of closing costs, which are payable at the closing or settlement meeting

Realtor: A real estate broker or an associate who holds an active membership in a local real estate board that is affiliated with the National Association of Realtors

Refinancing: Securing a new loan in order to pay off the existing mortgage or to gain access to the existing equity in the home

Roll-in Loan: A refinance loan that rolls any closing costs or fees into the loan. These programs best serve people who have a reasonable amount of equity, want to reduce their overall interest expense, and plan to stay in their homes

Rural Housing Service (RHS): The agency in the US Department of Agriculture providing financing to farmers and other qualified borrowers buying property in rural areas who are unable to obtain loans elsewhere. It offers low-interest-rate loans with no down payment to borrowers with low-to-moderate incomes who live in rural areas or small towns

Sales Agreement: A written contract signed by the buyer and the seller of a house stating the terms and conditions under which the property will be sold

Second Mortgage: A mortgage on the property that has a lien position behind the first mortgage

Servicer: An organization that collects monthly mortgage principal and interest payments from homeowners and manages escrow accounts for paying taxes and homeowners' insurance premiums The servicer often services mortgages that have been purchased by an investor in the secondary mortgage market

Settlement: See closing

Sub-prime Mortgage: A mortgage granted to a borrower considered sub-prime, that is, a person with a less-than perfect credit report. Sub-prime borrowers either have missed payments on a debt or have been late with payments. Lenders charge a higher interest rate to compensate for potential losses from customers who may run into trouble and default

Time is of the Essence: A phrase inserted in contracts to require a punctual performance

Title: A legal document proving a person's right to claim entitlement to a property, including the history of the property's ownership

Title Binder: Written evidence of temporary title insurance coverage

Title Company: A company that specializes in examining and insuring titles to real estate

Title insurance: Insurance that protects against loss from disputes over ownership of a property. A policy may protect the mortgage lender and/or the homebuyer

Title search: A check of title records to ensure that the seller is the legal owner of a property and that there are no liens or other claims against the property

Transfer Tax: State or local tax levied when title passes from one owner to another

Treasury Index: An index used to determine interest rate changes for certain ARM mortgages. It is based on the results of auctions that the US Treasury holds for its Treasury bills and securities or is derived from the US Treasury's daily yield curve, which is based on the closing market bid yields on actively traded Treasury securities in the over-the-counter market

Truth-in-Lending Act (TILA): A federal law that requires lenders to disclose, in writing, the terms and conditions of a mortgage, including the annual percentage rate APR and other charges

Underwriter: A company or person undertaking the responsibility for issuing a mortgage Underwriters analyze a borrower's credit worthiness and set the loan amount

VA Mortgage: A loan backed by the Veterans Administration. It requires very low or no down payments and has less stringent requirements for qualification. Members of the US armed forces are eligible for the loans under certain qualifying conditions

Wraparound Mortgage: A new mortgage that includes the remaining balance on the old mortgage plus a new amount

www.ingramcontent.com/pod-product-compliance
Lightning Source LLC
Chambersburg PA
CBHW081149270326
41930CB00014B/3092